THE SALEM WITCHES'
BOOK OF
LOVE SPELLS

THE SALEM WITCHES' BOOK OF LOVE SPELLS

♥ *Ancient Spells From Modern Witches*

Lilith McLelland

A Citadel Press Book
Published by Carol Publishing Group

A Citadel Press Book
Published by Carol Publishing Group
Citadel Press is a registered trademark of Carol Communications, Inc.

Editorial, sales and distribution, and rights and permissions inquiries should be addressed to Carol Publishing Group, 120 Enterprise Avenue, Secaucus, N.J. 07094

In Canada: Canadian Manda Group, One Atlantic Avenue, Suite 105, Toronto, Ontario M6K 3E7

Carol Publishing Group books may be purchased in bulk at special discounts for sales promotion, fund-raising, or educational purposes. Special editions can be created to specifications. For details, contact: Special Sales Department, Carol Publishing Group, 120 Enterprise Avenue, Secaucus, N.J. 07094.

Manufactured in the United States of America
10 9 8 7 6 5 4 3 2 1

Library of Congress Cataloging-in-Publication Data

McLelland, Lilith.
    The Salem witches' book of love spells : ancient spells from modern witches / Lilith McLelland.
        p.   cm.
    "A Citadel Press book."
    ISBN 0-8065-2020-5 (pbk.)
    1. Witchcraft. 2. Love—Miscellanea. 3. Magic. I. Title.
BF1572.L6M35   1998
133.4'42—dc21   98-21720
                                                   CIP

To
Kerowyn Silverdrake,
Warrior Woman, Dragon Keeper, Faithful Servant of the
Sacred Ratties and Guinea Pig Gods, without whose help
this book would never have been finished

Contents

1. The Basics of Love Spells   3

2. Aphrodisiacs and Love Potions: They're Good, and They're Good for You!   25

3. Pagan Love Secrets of the Gods   41

4. Friendship and Family Spells   76

5. Becoming More Lovable   90

6. Great Balls o' Fire! White Trash Love Spells   102

7. Historical Love Spells: Don't Try These at Home!   112

8. Anti-Love Spells: Taking the Off Ramp on the Highway of Love   125

9. The Myths and the Truth of Today's Witches: Step Back, Margaret Hamilton!   137

Covens, Groups, and Witches: Contributors to This Book   150

Reading List   152

The Salem Witches' Book of Love Spells

1

The Basics of Love Spells

I will show you a philtre without potions, without herbs,
without any witch's incantation: if you wish to be
loved, love.

—Seneca

Everyone wants just one thing from life: true love.

And money.

Okay, two things. But what we're concerned with here is love, and I'm talking True Love, All-Consuming Love, Love that transcends all earthly desires, not just some quickie spur-of-the-moment, backseat, I'll-respect-you-in-the-morning deal. (Not that that's a *bad* thing, which is why I've included a section on White Trash Love Spells.)

To find True Love, you should work on improving your personality, lose a few pounds, have your hair restyled, and maybe get a little cosmetic surgery or become real famous.

Please do *not* make me laugh.

You're going to lose weight when you're already putting away a quart of Ben & Jerry's every night because you're bored and lonely? And sometimes, all the surgical nip 'n' tuck in the world won't help—case in point: Cher. The poster girl for the Plastic Surgeon's Association, but look at some of the losers she hooked up with (although, I gotta admit, a lot of them were cute). As for getting famous: Beavis & Butthead have their own *movie* and they *still* can't score.

No, to attract love these days, you need more than old-fashioned openness and sharing and bribery. You need old-fashioned magic. Spells. Sorcery. Hoodoo. What you need is a friend in the business, if you get my drift. Somebody willing to share those shadowy secrets you've been hearing about. And you need somebody *good,* not somebody with a 900 number at five bucks a minute.

In this book, the Witches of Salem, Massachusetts, and their friends—an experienced group if ever there was one—share their favorite Love Spells, some of them dating back to colonial times. It wasn't unusual for a Salem couple in 1692 to produce ten kids. And how do you think Hester earned her scarlet **A**? Those Love Spells *worked!*

Why Do You Need A Love Spell?

Maybe you don't. But if you're looking through this book, you're probably interested in them, or just curious. Almost everyone can do with a little more love in his or her life, even if it's only more *self*-love and self-esteem.

The word *love* covers a lot of ground—not just romantic love. You can use Love Spells for:

A closer bond between lovers
More understanding between couples
Eliminating the strain between parents and kids
Finding the perfect mate, of course
Finding good friends
Becoming the kind of person who attracts love
Promoting all kinds of friendship
Earning and giving respect, even with people at work
Closer ties of understanding between siblings or friends
Enhancing those "romantic" evenings together

Love Rules

There are three basic rules to doing Love Spells. Follow them, and you'll really have a good time doing magic. You could enhance your life, your friendships, your self-confidence, and your love affairs, safely and happily. Break them, and you could find yourself in the kind of trouble you never dreamed existed.

1. The goal of your spell should be the best possible outcome of a situation.
2. Don't do anything that's going to screw around with the free will of others.
3. Make *absolutely* sure that the spell you're doing will cause no harm.

There's a good news and bad news in doing any kind of magic, especially Love Spells. And I'm going to give you the bad news first, so we can end later on a happier note.

How the Rules Work

What do you want? Why are you doing this spell? Are you doing it for the love of a specific person? If you are, you're asking for trouble. Spells are never done to produce a specific person: they're done to attract the right person for you, whoever that may be.

The first thing to keep in mind is that you never know who's out there for you. You might *think* you know, but I guarantee you that you don't. You can have the most accurate mental picture of the perfect mate, you can even have somebody specific in mind. Then you do a Love Spell for a hot date on Friday night and who shows up but that geek in accounting. So, having nothing else to do that night, you go out with him. And he turns out to be funny or charming or at least he says everything you've always wanted to hear. And against your better judgment—but thinking that maybe there's more to this guy than meets the eye—you go out with him again. Eventually you go to bed with him. And he turns out to be more than adequate. In fact, he turns out to be just *sensational*. In a very short time, Mr. Geek has proven himself to be Eros the Love God and you're walking around with this little secret, satisfied smile on your face because *who knew?*

The very best love matches are the "Damn! Who would have thought of it?" kind, the kind that surprise you because someone you never thought about romantically turned out to be just perfect.

So don't assume that you know who you want.

When it comes to love, you *never* know,

In fact, let's look at an all-too-typical case. Tristan has had a crush on Isolde for a long time. But Isolde is engaged to Tristan's friend Mark, and there don't seem to be any problems in the relationship. However, Tristan does a spell to win Isolde's love, and it works. She's all his.

Pretty soon, Isolde gets on Tristan's nerves. In the blinding light of his idealized love, he never noticed the way she tends to pout if she doesn't get her way. Her "little-girl charm" proved to be clingy dependency. And if he hears that annoying baby talk of hers one more time, he's gonna strangle her. Plus, he's no longer friends with Mark, and that's a loss he regrets. And Isolde: she's not all that happy, either. She and Tristan just aren't on the same wavelength, he finds fault with her all the time, and she can't figure out what's wrong.

But Tristan got what he wanted. Too bad he didn't think to do the spell for the perfect person for him—instead, he thought he *knew* that person was Isolde.

Another thing: Tristan's spell made three reasonably happy people into three miserable ones.

This is what happens when you "put spells on people" and that's why Witches never do it. Witches will do spells *for* people, if we know them well, but never any kind of spell that takes away a person's free will to choose his or her own actions.

Here's the difference. Doing a spell *for* someone is sending good thoughts and good wishes for the best possible outcome of a problem or situation. It's not unusual among Witches for someone to be going into the hospital and asking us, "Will you do some magic to speed up the healing?"

Even then, a lot of us are reluctant to do even that, unless the person is asking for him or herself. For instance, somebody's Aunt Griselda is sick and dying, and the nephew asks a Witch friend to do a spell to let her live. As cold as it sounds, a true Witch would refuse. Why? Because it might be Aunt Griselda's time to die. She might be in pain, or just plain ready to go, or maybe if she lives it means living a life of dependency and agony. Instead, the true Witch would do a spell for a peaceful transition for Aunt Griselda and the best possible outcome of her situation, and comfort for the grieving family.

Putting a spell "on" someone is trying to force that person to do something—not because *he* or *she* wants to, but because *you* want it. It's magic with evil intent, because it's totally selfish and the person doing it doesn't care who gets hurts.

All those spells you hear about involving someone's hair, fingernail parings, or personal items are bad magic. There's a heavy-duty price to be paid for doing magic like this. These spells, in greater or lesser degree, always cause harm. They may even work—in fact, they *do* work. But not always as you intended. And don't be thinking that you can get out of the penalty by saying, "But I didn't mean to hurt anyone!" You chose to do the spell, you chose to disregard the rule about harm, and you're responsible.

What goes around comes around, and sometimes it comes around real fast. Worst case scenario: You do a spell so that Mr. Wonderful will leave his wife and you two can be together forever. And you *are* together forever because you're both killed in a car crash and nobody can tell whose burnt charred remains are whose. If this sounds too gruesome, believe me, things like this happen when you start fooling around with black magic. I have never—*never*—known anyone using black magic who didn't have it come back on him or her. And every one of them thought they were clever enough to control it. Right up until the moment it jumped up and grabbed them by the throat.

None of the spells in this book are black magic except the ones in the chapter about historical Love Spells, which are included because they're interesting, and those are not spells you could actually perform anyway. Some of them are so totally gross that they're funny, and one of them takes the award for the Most Disgusting Love Spell in History.

Don't Be a Good Samaritan

While doing good deeds for others is a fine rule to follow in life, it isn't so great in magic and spells. When you start doing spells for other people, you can very easily fall into the trap of thinking that you know what's best for all concerned.

You don't. You have no idea of the karmic implications of others' actions. For instance: Your sister and her husband squabble all the time. They're driving you nuts, plus it bothers you a lot that they don't seem to get along better when they're both such nice people. So you decide to do a spell to make them stop bickering.

Okay, right off the bat, you're doing a spell to *force* someone to do something. Not great. It might sound like a nice idea, but you're meddling in the affairs of other people's karma. They might be arguing all the time because they've got some things they have to work out between themselves, one way or another, and this is the way it's got to happen. And, to tell the truth, they may *like* squabbling: this might be the way that both of them let off steam. A woman in my coven, famous for quibbling with her boyfriend, told me "Couples who don't bicker are headed for *trouble!*" and the boyfriend wholeheartedly agreed. They're still together, still happy and still bickering. Once their friends understood this, it actually became kind of amusing.

So if you do your sweetness-and-light spell, you're interfering with the process. And you don't know how that "make them stop fighting" spell will work out. Two people fight. Remove one of them and the fight's over. Think about those implications.

Here's where you have to think things through. You can't do a spell to make them do anything, but you can do a spell—and only with their full cooperation—to enhance understanding between them, to help them resolve their differences with the best possible outcome. Provided they have differences in the first place.

Love Spells done for other people can work out badly too. You don't know precisely what other people need, and you don't know if one of the parties involved is lying about the relationship—to him or herself as much as to you. Witches cringe when asked to do Love Spells, and we never do them for people we don't know. Most of us won't do them at all for anyone except ourselves.

Do your own spells, take your own responsibility, is our motto.

Spell Insurance

I like to end all my spells with the words, "This spell is done with harm to none." That way, nobody gets hurt. If you've inadvertently worded a spell wrong or done it wrong, this little incantation assures that the spell will not work if any harm accrues to it.

It won't hurt or invalidate any of the spells in this book if you add that Spell Insurance to it. The butt you save may be your own.

The Good News

Okay, now that the warnings are out of the way . . .

Doing magic is fun, and everyone has the power to do it. Everyone's born with magical power in equal amounts. The reason Witches seem so good at it is because we get lots of practice.

Another reason is that we believe in magic. Either we never paid attention to the conventional wisdom that says that magic doesn't exist, or we relearned the habit of getting what we want.

And before you say, "Then why don't Witches win the Lottery?" let me reassure you that many of us have. A friend of mine just won sixty mil in his state lottery. He was a fairly happy Witchy before, but now . . . woo*hoo!*

Gay Love Spells

Most of the spells in this book were written with a heterosexual slant because most of the people who contributed were straight. But there's absolutely no reason that any of these spells can't work as well gay as straight. Love is love, and if love between consenting and horny adults makes the world a little better, who cares if it's gay or straight? If you get your panties twisted over what other people are doing in bed, then you'd better get somebody to pry that house off your sister, grab your cheap ruby slippers, and get outta Oz.

What Magic Is and How It Works

I'm going to tell you what I believe about magic, its effects, and what causes those effects. Whether *you* believe it or not is up to you, naturally, but a basic understanding of the Witch's view of magic is essential when doing any kind of spellwork.

A spell isn't a recipe. You don't just mix the proper ingredients and—poof—magic happens. Actually, it's more like Frankenstein. The good doctor had all the parts, he put them together in the right order, but he couldn't make his creation live. Not until he had tapped into that electric spark of life that could only be provided by the universe. Witches doing magic are tapping into that source. And, like Frankenstein's monster, if it isn't done in the right spirit and without the intent to do harm, magic can turn on you.

Aleister Crowley once said that magic is the manipulation of natural law by the will in order to cause change. While I don't usually agree with Crowley, I do agree with him there. Like many other magicians and philosophers and modern psychiatrists, he believed that the power of the mind, the will, was strong enough to bring about changes in the physical world.

Everyone knows that you can "think" yourself sick, and that in some cases you can also "think" yourself better; the right attitude can produce certain chemicals in the brain and body to fight illness. I believe in healing by faith—as long as you also get some competent medical help. But magic and faith and positive thinking can push that medical help along, with sometimes amazing results.

You can also think yourself into and out of social situations. In an extreme case, we have the battered wife. Not that her situation is her fault by any means, but if she maintains the attitude (usually carefully instilled in her by her husband) that she "deserves" it, she'll never get out of that situation. On the other hand, if that mental pattern is broken and she starts thinking of herself as stronger, she's on her way to taking action and getting out. That's why abusers take such care to keep their victims ashamed, confused, and guilty by telling the abused, "I love you so much, honey, that I just want you to be perfect, and that's why I have to discipline you. If you'd straighten out, I wouldn't have to do this. You *make* me do it." If he can get his partner to buy into this—and he usually does—he wins.

The woman can do a spell to help her out of this, but it isn't the stones, or the crystals, or the spoken incantation that does it: It's the reinforcement of her own will, the strength of her determination. That determination is a decision to connect herself into the natural laws, into God or the Higher Power or the Universal Mind or whatever you want to call it. She can tap into that strength and use it.

Magic is the connection with the universal power that's out there, that governs natural law, that makes the spark of life from an inanimate body. Witches believe it's this connection to their God and Goddess that make magic work. Some psychics claim it's guardian spirits. Christians say it's Jesus or God turning water into wine and such. Whatever you choose to believe, there *is* something out there and you can assign any name to it that you want. You can simply accept it, or build an elaborate religion around it, or ignore it: It still exists.

But you're part of it and so is everyone and everything else, bad or good. Like a spider web that has many, many strands making up the whole. And because you're connected, what you do affects everything else.

Magic works in easy, almost unnoticed ways. It looks a lot like coincidence. You do a spell for, say, a better computer. Does a new computer appear at your door? Only in fairy tales, babe. What happens is that a friend gets a new computer and offers you his old one real cheap, which is better than yours by a long shot. Or you luck into some money or a temporary job which lets you buy a new computer. It all looks coincidental, but it happened at exactly the right time.

Magic has no idea of "good" or "bad" or "black" or "white." It just exists, like any other force of nature. If you're doing good things with it, or you're doing bad, you're using the same force. Like electricity it can be harnessed to a life-saving machine, or it can power the electric chair. Does electricity make its choice between bad and good use? Hardly. That's your job, and that's where free will comes in. You make the choice, you take the consequences for the bad ones.

Free will is an essential part of what Witches call the Threefold Law of Karma: What you do comes back to you three times.

If you're doing good, good comes back to you three times. If you're doing evil, that also comes back three times. It works in everyday life as well as in magic. This is why Witches never have to do revenge spells. Why should we bring that kind of karma on ourselves when the wrongdoer will bring retribution on himself? And the longer it takes to happen, the harder it will be. You've undoubtedly seen people get away with stuff you wouldn't *believe,* and you wonder why nothing bad happens to them. Don't worry, it will. When it'll do the most good.

Karma isn't punishment, however; karma is the universe's way of teaching us lessons. Sometimes they're easy lessons, sometimes they're harsh. The Romans had a wonderful goddess for this: Nemesis, the Goddess of Retribution and Righteous Anger. Nemesis had no definite form. No one knew what she looked like. Instead, she manifested herself in people who served to teach hard lessons to wrongdoers. The people were totally innocent, but in their innocence, they became the instruments of Nemesis, against whom no untruth or injustice could stand. If you'd done evil, you'd never know who was going to be your Nemesis.

Psychic power or magic power, whatever you want to call it, is a matter of the mind and will. You want something to happen, you concentrate on it, and you connect yourself with the universal powers to get it done. The stronger your will and your concentration, the more likely it is that the work will happen the way you want it to. Everyone has psychic power, everyone is born with it. It's just that most of us have rationalized and civilized it out of our consciousness. That doesn't mean it isn't still there.

Spells work because the crystals, the colors, the herbs, the "things" connected with the spells all serve to focus your complete attention on what you're doing. The spoken parts of spells confirm and strengthen your will. Sure, the crystals, herbs, colors, and all the rest have their own magical meanings and properties, which help things along, but believe me: that's a popgun compared to the cannon blast that is the individual mind.

Of course there's a catch to this, and that catch is that you must be in control of your mind and your power of concentration. But there's a technique for it: Read on.

Using the Mind for Magic: Preparation for Spellwork

First of all, you have to be quiet. And if you think that's easy in today's society, just try it for a while. Traffic noise, the radio, TV, stereo, the phone ringing—it seems as though we just can't live without noise. Whether we hear it directly or subliminally, it distracts us from our thoughts and makes true concentration impossible.

And, wouldn't you know it, that intense concentration is just what you must have to do magic. It's the only thing that is *absolutely* necessary to the process. You can dispense with everything else, but you must have the concentration that exists only in silence.

Witches have a saying: *In silence is the seed of wisdom gained.* The psychic information we get comes out of that silence, and the ability to analyze and apply that information is processed when we have the time and the quiet to do it.

These days, if you're going to get a little peace and quiet, you're going to have to make it for yourself. So here's a technique for meditation and mild self-hypnosis that you can use to calm your mind.

Find a time and place where you can be alone and quiet. No TV, no music, not even that "New Age" meditation jelly brain music. Sit comfortably and relax. Close your eyes. Then start breathing; take a deep breath and let it out slowly. Do this two or three times to warm up, then do it three or four more times. As you breathe out, feel all the tenseness and troubles melt off

you, like wax off a candle. Don't worry if your mind is chatter-
ing away at you—it does that. But as you relax and breathe, listening to your breathing, your mind will calm down. You'll be
ready to concentrate on whatever task you've set yourself.

Open your eyes slowly, get accustomed to the room around
you, and let yourself feel good for a minute, with no worries.
Even if troubles are besetting you on all sides, give yourself
these few minutes in which nothing happens and nothing in-
trudes. A small space of time to yourself isn't going to make
your problems any worse, but it can sure make you better able
to cope. Think of it as a psychic vacation.

It's in this state that you should do your magic spells.

Gather everything together first, all the ingredients, all the
things you'll need. Then do whatever the spell involves: writing
things, reading an incantation, braiding a cord, putting incense
together. While you're doing that, concentrate on what you want
the spell to accomplish. After you've put everything together, do
this relaxation technique again and really concentrate on what
you've just done and what you want. If your spell involves an
incantation, do the relaxation just before you read it, and let all
your mind and will focus on it. For that space of time, nothing
else should be going on in your mind except what you're doing.
Most important, don't do the spell until you have the time.

The stronger your power of concentration, the stronger the
spell will be.

Many Witches don't even bother to do formal spells. We
think about the problem, we ask the gods for advice or information, then go into a meditative state to hear what the gods
have to say to us. But this takes experience and practice.

Magical Tools

The spells in this book vary, but many of them contain at least
one of the four indispensable tools used by Witches: *the Witch's*

Cord, the Witch's Scent, the Fire Spell, and the Conjure Bag. The ingredients and spells attached to these tools are all different, but the technique is the same. To some I've added a fifth tool: Spirit Incense. The incense is especially important when working with the gods and spirits—it's not only a magical tool, but an offering to the spirits and gods, invoking and thanking them for their help.

The basic instructions for each tool follows. Specific instructions are included with each spell.

The Witch's Cord

These are beautiful, fun to make, and magically very powerful. In the old days, they were called Witch's Ladders. The basic idea is that you take three lengths of cord, ribbon, string, yarn ... whatever ... and charge them with your magical intentions. You can braid them together, which is the usual procedure, or you can take the historical route, which is to tie nine knots in all three cords, treating the three lengths as one. At each knot, make a wish relating to the purpose of the cord, or repeat the spell or incantation you're doing.

The three colors of the cord should represent the kind of magic you want done: there will be a color chart later; watch for it—you'll love it.

When you've got the cord braided or knotted, you can use it just like it is, or if you want to get elaborate, you can tie or glue other magical things into the cord for more power.

Witch's Cords are left hanging in your house, drawing magic power into themselves and into the house and your life.

Witch's Scents

Aromatherapy is now becoming très chic among the New Age set, but Witches have always known about the mood-enhancing and mood-changing properties of scents. Certain scents were also thought to have magical powers and to be associated with various gods, goddesses, and spirits.

Essential oils provide the finest, most effective scents, because of their purity. You'll want to use the best oils you can afford, but don't go off the deep end. Pure rose essence, for instance, is incredibly expensive since to make a dram of it requires twenty-five thousand rose petals and a lot of time. Synthetic rose oil is just as good. So is synthetic ambergris, which is probably going to be all you can find, since ambergris comes from whales, and is actually kind of unpleasant in its raw state. Both these scents are very common to Love Spells.

The *Witch's Scent Jar* is designed for one person to use while doing magic. Dab the scented oil on a cotton ball and place the ball in a small glass jar or bottle with a lid or a stopper or cork. When you want to use the fragrance, just open the jar and hold it under your nose and enjoy the beautiful scent while you chant your spell. To tell what oil to use, just look at the ingredient list of the spells in each chapter and pick your favorite fragrance.

If you want scents for two, use lightbulb rings, aromatherapy lamps, a few drops of scented oils in water simmered in a potpourri simmering lamp or in a small pot over a very, very low burner on the stove. The fabulous fragrances will fill your house, creating a romantic, magic mood.

Use an eyedropper to smolder a few drops of scented oils on charcoal (see *Incense,* below). For this, you're going to definitely want essential oils rather than synthetics, since some synthetics smell great in the bottle and in the aromatherapy lamps or lightbulb rings, but when smoldered on charcoal, they give off the unforgettable aroma of burning tires. So unless *Essence de Auto Junkyard* is the effect you're going for, use the best oils.

Fire Spells

There are two kinds of Fire Spells, both as hypnotic as they are effective.

In the first kind of Fire Spell, you write your spell on a piece of paper and burn it.

Naturally, you can dress it up a lot more than that, but it's the act of concentrating your energies into the writing of the spell, then the hypnotic act of watching the flames as it burns that does the magic.

If you have a fireplace or you're doing this outdoors—over a hibachi, for example—then you have no problem. If you'd like to do it indoors and you have no fireplace, you'll have to be a little more careful.

In any case, the piece of paper you're using should be plain paper, no writing or printing on it except the spell, and should be no bigger than a standard 8½ × 11 sheet. Smaller is actually better, if you're working indoors, because of the flame-control factor.

Burn your spell away from anything flammable—like furniture—in a large pot, turkey roasting pan, or other metal container, and be sure it's on a fireproof, heatproof surface, such as a large trivet (I have a twelve-inch ceramic tile). I know one Witch who used a nice copper caldron to burn her spells, which was fine except that she set it on the synthetic living room carpet, which promptly melted from the heat. (Unlike the pope, Witches are *not* infallible.)

Personally, I think indoor Fire Spells are best done in the kitchen, near a big jar of water or a fire extinguisher.

In the second kind of Fire Spell, called Scented Fire, you're not burning the written spell. You're speaking your spell, then concentrating on the fire. The act of watching the fire hypnotizes you into connecting with your own psychic power, thus making your magical intentions more effective. The reason it's called Scented Fire is that you use essential oils corresponding to the kind of magic you're doing.

Scented Fire needs 91 percent rubbing alcohol, which burns better than any other, and a small—and I emphasize *small*—metal bowl or pot sitting securely on a non-flammable surface.

And you'd better be sure it's nonflammable because the bowl gets very hot very fast. Do not touch it again until the fire's out and enough time has passed for the bowl to cool.

To make Scented Fire, add a few drops of essential oils to about a tablespoonful of alcohol, then quickly touch a match to the alcohol, which will flame up high and fast. It will burn long enough for you to recite your spell and concentrate on what you want as you watch the flames. After the flame dies out, the heated oil will release a gentle, smoke-free fragrance.

Again, these two spells are ones you might want to stay away from if you have cats. Or, assuming you're the clumsy type, if you want to keep your eyebrows.

Conjure Bags

These are a time-honored tradition, especially in New Orleans, where they're known as Mojo Bags or Gris-Gris Bags. You put whatever magical ingredients you're using into a small bag and tie it with string or cord. You can carry it with you, give it to someone, hang it in your car or house, hang it over your door-way, or do whatever else is appropriate. (If you live in New Orleans and you're doing bad magic, you'd bury it under someone's doorstep—and eventually take the consequences.)

Conjure Bags are made in specific colors according to the magic you're doing. For instance, if you're doing a spell for romantic passion, red is always a strong color. The bags don't have to be actual bags, although you can buy little drawstring bags already made up, in lots of colors. The bags we're talking about in this book are simply squares of colored fabric. You put the magical ingredients into the center of the square, draw up the corners, and tie them with a piece of cord or string, leaving enough to make a loop for hanging.

You can get fancy with these, too, adding beads, feathers or crystals and using metallic cord and fancy fabrics if you want.

Just plain colored cotton fabric works just as well. It's magical intent that counts.

Conjure Bags work very well tied onto Witch's Cords.

Incense

Incense is one of the oldest of magical tools. The scented smoke carries its own power, and infuses the area with magical vibrations. In ancient times, the Sybils, prophetic priestesses, burned hallucinogenic incense to increase their psychic powers. Incense was used in offerings to the gods to invoke their aid. Native Americans burn sage, cedar, and grasses and herbs to "smudge" an area, purging it of harmful energies and creating a neutral space in which to work magic. Many Christian denominations use incense the same way, especially frankincense and myrrh.

You can use ordinary stick or cone incense in your spells, if you like. This is certainly the easiest way to do it.

But, if you really want to get ambitious, make your own. It's not all that difficult, since the incense we'll be using consists of loose herbs, spices, or resins. Specific incense recipes are included in the spells.

General Rules for Making and Using Incense

Mix all the dry ingredients together in a glass jar or bowl—never plastic or metal; those surfaces affect the scent of the oils, especially over time—then add the oils a drop or two at a time, mixing thoroughly. Store unused incense in glass bottles or jars.

When you've made your incense, you smolder it by sprinkling a teaspoonful or so at a time on glowing charcoal embers.

You can't use plain old backyard BBQ charcoal for this. Instead you need the kind of charcoal used in church, which isn't hard to find and it's cheap—about two dollars for five large pieces or ten small ones. It comes rolled in foil. Any church supply store will have it, and so will your local New Age store or herb shop. The charcoal is round, about a half inch thick, and about an inch in diameter, with a little round "well" in the center to hold the incense.

It's self-lighting. Hold it over a candle flame using ice tongs or something similar, moving the charcoal back and forth while it catches; do not even *try* to do this with your fingers! There'll be a shower of beautiful golden sparks to tell you it's catching. It won't flame up itself, so don't expect it to catch fire. Set it in whatever holder you're using. When the charcoal's glowing, or has built up a fine layer of gray ash, it's ready for you to spoon the incense on it.

The charcoal will generate heat, but the best way I've found to make sure that tabletops and surfaces aren't harmed is to fill a Pyrex or ceramic or pottery bowl *at least* five inches in diameter with sand or dirt and set the charcoal on the sand. You can buy little brass holders for the charcoal, but they're going to get very hot and they're sometimes unstable, so I prefer the bowl. The sand offsets the heat and adds stability to the bowl; you don't want this thing tipping over. I've found that romantic interludes are rarely enhanced when the curtains or the bed catch fire, so you might want to plan ahead. Also, there's smoke involved here, so either have adequate ventilation or move the incense away from the smoke detectors. And if you have curious cats who can jump, you might want to rethink the entire incense ritual anyway and use some other form of magic, like aromatic oils that don't have to be smoldered.

Spoon some incense into the little well in the charcoal, and the scented smoke will start to rise, filling the room with magic.

Note that it doesn't burn: it *smolders*. If you're doing this with someone else, make sure that person isn't allergic to smoke. Incense doesn't contain the irritants that cigarette smoke does, but it's still smoke.

Store charcoal in a dry place, or in a glass jar with a tight-fitting lid. Once it gets damp, it never really dries out and it's useless.

Charging

This is merely telling the ingredient in a spell what you want it to do. As you'll notice throughout this book, many substances have more than one magical property: lavender, for instance, can be used both to attract love and to banish it. So, as you're adding ingredients to your spell or incense or Conjure Bag, just mention what you want it to do, such as, "Lavender, I charge you to attract a lover to me."

Color and Magic

For centuries, certain colors were thought to be either powerful in their own right, or to enhance magical working by attracting the correct powers and spirits. There were even said to heal, something that's being proved today with the psychological studies of the effects of color on behavior and mood. Oddly enough, a calming bubble-gum pink is supposed to work well in violent wards of hospitals, and in prisons, something I'm not sure would appeal to the criminal mind.

There is, as usual in magic lore, a wide interpretation of the meanings of various colors, but here are some of the most common. Use them when making Conjure Bags or Witch's Cords, writing spells, making talismans, or anywhere else that color can lend a magical hand.

Color	Meaning
Red	Renewal and rebirth, romantic love, courage, passion
Pink	Friendship, affection, self-love
Bright blue	Good luck, healing
Gold or yellow	The sun, happiness, success, faithful friends
Purple, lavender	Psychic visions and dreams, peace
Orange	Wisdom
Green	Growth, money, nature
Black, dark blue	Secrets, the night
Silver	The moon, magic, dreams
White	Protection, banishes fear

Love Stones and Crystals

Most of these stones have many other meanings and powers, but I'm listing only their uses in Love magic, since that's what we're concerned with here. This is merely an overview: it is by no means a complete list of the magical meanings of stones, minerals, and crystals. That's a study in itself, and a fascinating one. But this chart gives you a good start on the basics.

Stone	Magical Properties
Amber	Attracts love, success, increases attractiveness, protection
Amethyst	Peace, psychic power, good luck, attracts women
Blue lace agate	Peace
Citrine	Success, happiness
Hematite	Calming and healing, emotional healing

Stone	Magical Properties
Malachite	Wealth and love. Good for marrying money. Especially effective wrapped in copper, a metal sacred to Venus
Moonstone	Attracting and keeping love
Clear quartz	All-purpose magical stone: protection, healing, dreams, psychic power
Rose quartz	Friendship, affection, self-esteem, attracts men
Blue quartz	Peace and calm
Sunstone	Success, happiness, physical energy
Tiger's eye	Good luck, courage
Turquoise	Love, friendship, healing, good luck

And there you have the basic techniques and information for working the spells in this book. Have a good time, enjoy doing the spells and rituals, but above all, remember old Seneca's advice, which is the most effective Love Spell of all: If you would be loved, *love*.

2

Aphrodisiacs and Love Potions: They're Good, and They're Good for You!

When I fancy someone I always sleep with them. Oh,
I have to drug them first, of course, being so old
and warty . . .
—Curtis and Elton, *BlackAdder*

There's this lingering mystique about aphrodisiacs and love potions: after only one taste the beloved becomes mad with passion for the person who administered the aphrodisiac, and cannot rest until he or she physically possesses that person. One sip of the potion, one glance, one errant touch of a hand, and ripped-off clothes and inhibitions fly across the room like tossed confetti, amid moans of forbidden, secret pleasures undreamed-of among normal mortals.

As *if.*

Aphrodisiacs can never magically take the place of love, affection, or respect. And—all the high school nonsense about Spanish fly aside—aphrodisiacs cannot induce burning, undying passion. However, the right aphrodisiac used in the right way and at the right time can certainly enhance the feelings that are there.

Certain substances have a very long and honorable history as aphrodisiacs, some with the most fascinating folklore attached to them. Certainly no aphrodisiac is associated with more magical lore than the mandrake root. Oysters are famous for their potency-enhancing qualities. And chocolate was thought to be such a powerful libidinous stimulant that it was banned by the Church (but then, so was just about everything that was any real fun).

And speaking of the Church, a number of those early monks apparently found a lot of loopholes in the vows of chastity, because some of our most reliable information on aphrodisiacs comes from the good brothers. One order, the monks of Saint Hyacinthe, was so accomplished at the art of love that a little sign was posted on the monastery, proving that it pays to advertise:

> *You ladies who for pregnancy do wish,*
> *To great Saint Hyacinthe your prayers apply,*
> *And what his Saintship cannot accomplish,*
> *The monks within will surely satisfy.*

Those wacky guys! I guess there's just something about a man in uniform.

Love Potions:
How to Make a Basic Potion

Potions, despite the mystical lore surrounding them, are very easy to make and use. The first thing to remember is that you *don't drink them*—at least, not the ones in this book. Making a potion is a lot like making an incense, only you're steeping the herbs in water.

Use about a cup of water in a small pot, preferably a pot you use only for potion-making, but we won't be picky here. While the water simmers (never hot enough to boil) add the ingredients one at a time, charging each one for its magical purpose. After all the ingredients are in and simmering for a few minutes, you can speak aloud the spell you're using, or simply state the purpose you want the potion to fulfill.

When the potion's cool, pour it through a strainer into a nice jar or bottle. You can get as plain or pretty with this as you like, even adding a few drops of food coloring in whatever color is appropriate to the spell you're doing. Potions in pretty bottles with ribbons tied around them and a crystal or two in the bottle make nice little presents.

Potions are dabbed onto Witch's Cords or Conjure Bags, onto the paper when you use written spells, sprinkled around a room (usually into the four corners) or across a doorway, or sprinkled sparingly and discreetly onto bedlinens—but if you're coloring the potion, guard against stains. Small dram bottles of potions are also good to hang from the Witch's Cords.

❤ Salem Witch's Love Potion #9¾

If you're a Witch in Salem, Massachusetts, and some visitor comes up to talk to you, you can pretty much bet that among the first five questions will be, "Do you have any love potions?"

As a matter of fact, I do! This is the famous love potion everyone asks us about. Use it in conjunction with a spoken spell to bring the perfect person for you into your life, to enhance the love you already have between the two of you (or, three, if you're inclined that way) and for love and friendship. Many of the Witches in Salem like to sprinkle this around their rooms and dab it on the front and back doors of their houses, to promote a general feeling of friendship for all who enter. Of course, if you get a lot of Jehovah's Witnesses at your door, you might want to turn them away, but at least you'll all feel friendly about it.

1 teaspoon rose petals, red or pink, both is better. Charge
the red rose petals for passionate love and for feminine
energy; charge the pink petals for friendship and
affection

1 teaspoon lavender, for attracting love to you

½ teaspoon oak leaves or bark, for strength and for masculine
energy

A few dashes cinnamon, for magic power and success in love

All simmered in 2 cups of water

While you're brewing this, repeat this spell:

*By the powers of the Goddess and God, by the power of Aphrodite
and Venus, by all the good spirits of love, I charge this incense to
attract love, good feelings, romance, passionate love between lovers,
affection, and lasting friendship. This spell is done with harm to none.*

Love From the Sea

There are two ways to look at seafood and passion. One, the
more romantic view, states that Venus, the Goddess of Love,
was born of the sea, so that all sea creatures share in her magical qualities.

The other view, not so romantic unless you're a chemist, has
to do with phosphorus and brain chemistry.

I like to think that the combination of the two—divine magic
and chemistry—is what makes seafood so effective. That stuff
about oysters? All true. Why do you think New Orleans is such
a romantic town? Because there's an oyster bar on practically
every street.

Oysters have a long history as an aid to love. The Roman
writer Apuleius married a rich widow, whose father accused him
of having used sorcery and magical charms to win the lady. The
love potion in question was supposed to have been made of
shellfish, lobsters, spiced oysters, and cuttlefish. Apuleius doesn't

say whether they ended the evening with a nice chocolate cake, but I'm betting that was on the menu, too.

And while we're considering fish as aphrodisiacs, let's not forget fowl. The celebrated magician Albertus Magnus recommended "the brains of a partridge, calcined into powder and swallowed in red wine." But if you're not big on powdered partridge brains, another Roman, Platina, favored plain old roasted partridge, which he said "strengthens the brain [*these guys had a thing for brains*], facilitates conception, and arouses the half-extinct desire for venereal pleasures." *Venereal pleasures* being the old phrase for the pleasures of Venus, and I'm sure we all know what those are.

A few of the ancients also recommended liver as a stimulant to love. They don't say what kind of liver or how to serve it, but some people like it with fava beans and a nice Chianti.

Mushrooms and truffles are also supposed to be terrific aphrodisiacs.

So the moral of this story is: If you want to get lucky, both of you should go out for a romantic dinner of partridge stuffed with mushrooms and truffles, a dozen smoked oysters, and a little liver on the side.

I'd hold the powdered partridge brains, however.

Mandrake

This is one of the earliest acknowledged aphrodisiacs, spoken of in ancient Greece and Rome, and even in the Song of Solomon. Mandrake is a root, shaped vaguely like the human figure, and is supposed to be of either male or female gender, depending on the look of the root. Lots of ancient spells call for either a male or female mandrake or a combination of the two.

Even getting your hands on mandrake root has all kinds of mystical restrictions: The root must be pulled out of the earth at the dark of the moon by tying the visible part of the plant to a dog, then letting the dog pull up the root. Finding the plant isn't simple, either: Mandrakes with the most magical power are supposedly those that grow under a gallows, in ground moistened by the semen of a hanged man. Eeeuuuwww.

Lady Elizabeth Woodville was accused of bewitching Edward IV into marriage by using a love potion made of mandrake. Never mind that she was totally gorgeous, it was the love potion and an accusation of witchcraft that sticks in the history books. In the fifteenth century, mandrake was so respected as an erotic stimulant that Machiavelli wrote about it in a satire called *La Mandragola, mandragola* being another name for mandrake.

However, if prepared by inexpert hands, the mandrake love potions were killers—literally. There are plenty of historical records of potential lovers dying or going insane from mandrake poisoning. Or just plain exhaustion.

But in this book, we're not giving anyone anything to drink or sprinkle on food (except the Chocolate Spells, naturally), so our Mandrake Love Spells are fairly safe.

Just remember to pace yourself. Like Groucho said, "I like my cigar, too, but I take it out once in a while."

♥ *Mandrake Conjure Bag for Passion*

You can use the power of mandrake for the excitement of passion with your present lover. Keep it near the bed or hang it on a Witch's Cord. Follow the general directions for bags in chapter 1. Your bag should be red for passion and tied with gold cord or string for success and happiness. Into the bag, put:

A small piece of mandrake, charged for passionate love
1 piece carnelian, charged for sexual power
Small piece of paper with this spell written in red ink:

By the fiery powers of the gods of love, I make this charm to rekindle in us the fires of passionate love. This spell is done with harm to none.

♥ Mandrake Conjure Bag for Love

If it's the sweet comfort of love you want, try this version of the mandrake bag. You'll want to carry this bag around with you, or hang it on a Witch's Cord. Follow the general directions for bags in chapter 1. Your bag should be pink for love, and tied with gold cord or string for success and happiness. Into the bag, put:

A small piece of mandrake, charged for bringing love
1 piece rose quartz, charged for love
Small piece of paper with this spell written in pink (for love) or black ink:

By the power of the spirits of love, I make this charm to attract love to me, to bring the perfect lover for me into my life, for the happiness of us both. This spell is done with harm to none.

♥ Witch's Cord With Mandrake

Follow the general directions for making Witch's Cords. If you're doing a cord for passion with your present lover, use two red strands and one gold strand and hang the Passion Conjure Bag from the finished cord. Charge the cord for bringing passion. If you intend the spell for love, use two pink strands and one gold one, attach the Love Conjure Bag, and charge the cord for attracting love.

♥ Mandrake Incense for Passionate Love

1 tablespoon powdered or chopped mandrake root, charged for passion
1 teaspoon cinnamon, for male energy

1 teaspoon rose, for female energy
10 drops of rose oil, charged for passion and love

When you've made the incense, use this spell to charge it:

> *Mandrake and cinnamon, heart of the rose,*
> *As your scent fills the air, so our sweet passion grows.*

♥ *Mandrake Passion Potion*

Use the same ingredients as the Mandrake Incense for Passion, leaving out the rose oil, and steep everything in water according to the general directions in chapter 1. If you like, you can *lightly* tint the finished potion with red food coloring. Charge the potion with this spell, which is like the incense spell—only different:

> *Mandrake and cinnamon, heart of the rose,*
> *Where I sprinkle this potion, our sweet passion grows.*

You'll want to spritz the stuff around the bedroom, especially in the four corners of the room, and dab a little on the headboard of the bed.

Amber and Ambergris

Another pair of ancient aphrodisiacs. You're probably more familiar with amber as that beautiful, golden solidified resin with insects trapped inside. But before it solidifies, amber resin is soft and crumbly and has a fascinatingly sweet scent, a little like vanilla. It's absolute catnip to men (actually, so is a little vanilla), and perfumes that contain real amber essence can be expensive. But worth it. Amber oil, worn as a perfume, is also a lovely way to attract men—just don't slather yourself in it; most oils are so concentrated that the barest touch to the pulse points is more than enough. Any perfume that overpowers, worn by men or women, usually has the opposite aphrodisiac effect. It's the suggestion, the mysterious breath of the scent, that intrigues.

The quality of amber oils varies, so sniff a few before you buy. And make sure it's pure, not fake amber essence.

The wearing of amber jewelry is also thought to attract love, so invest in those beautiful strings of beads, girlfriends. Men can wear cufflinks or a tie pin set with amber. Both sexes can carry a small piece of amber in a pocket.

Ambergris is another story. Real ambergris comes from whales and is kind of unpleasant in its concentrated form. It takes a master perfumer to control the scent, which is another reason that perfumes containing it are expensive. Artificial ambergris oils can be very appealing when blended into perfume oils; they're much less costly and just as magically effective.

Ambergris also has a long reputation as a love potion and a rejuvenator of jaded lovers. Madame du Barry used it as a stimulant to perk up Louis XV of France, who was getting a little too pooped to party—if you know what I mean. Madame called it *poudre de joie,* powder of joy. I don't even want to know what part she powdered down, but as Mel Brooks would say, "It's *good* to be the king!"

♥ *Amber Mist Incense*

If you want a really beautiful scent for love, you just can't beat amber. If you're using a powdered amber resin, just crumble a little on the smoldering charcoal. I also recommend premade amber stick or cone incense, and the best (in my opinion) is Amber Flame by Escential Essences.

If you're going to make your own incense, use the best amber essence oil you can find. Use about a tablespoon of powdered sandalwood for the base and add six to ten drops of amber oil and mix thoroughly. Let this mixture sit for a couple of days. Charge the amber for love, and the sandalwood to drive out any negative or harmful energies that would stand in the way of love.

Both of the following incenses can be used when you've invited the guy or girl of your dreams over for the evening and want to set a romantic mood. Or burn either of them while you're doing other spells to attract the perfect man or perfect woman for you. Remember to charge each ingredient as you add it.

♥ Amber/Ambergris Incense to Attract Men

Basically the same incense as Amber Mist, but use a little less amber oil, and add a few drops of ambergris oil to please a guy of the male gender.

♥ Amber/Musk Incense to Attract Women

Same as Amber Mist but leave out the ambergris oil and substitute patchouli or musk oil. Watch the proportions. There are so many brands of musk and patchouli oils in varying concentrations, that you might want to mix up a couple of test batches and try them out before the Big Night. When you've got it the way you want it, burn it and become a Babe Magnet.

♥ Ancient Amber Incense

This is a love potion recipe from 1588. The actual recipe is so detailed and the measures and procedures so archaic that to duplicate it would be very difficult, unless you were either a chemist or a distiller. But the basic ingredients make a lovely incense.

1 tablespoon sandalwood base, charged for good luck
1 teaspoon amber or 10 drops of amber oil, charged for love
1 teaspoon powdered musk or 5 drops musk oil, charged
   for sensuality
1 teaspoon aloe powder, for strength
¼ teaspoon cinnamon, for passion
½ teaspoon dried orange peel, for happiness
5 drops of rose oil, in honor of Venus, Goddess of Love

Use this incense in conjunction with other love spells. It's good for attracting love, for friendship, for sensuality, for happiness: for almost anything connected with love.

♥ *Ancient Amber Love Oil*

If you want to make the above recipe into a Love Oil to wear, add only the oils to about ¼ cup of almond oil as a base. Don't add the aloe or sandalwood powder, and substitute cinnamon and orange oil instead of the regular cinnamon and orange— just a few drops, because both these oils have strong scents. In the case of cinnamon oil, be very careful because it can irritate the skin if used full strength.

After you've made the perfume, charge it for whatever love purpose you wish. Or wear it while you're doing your love spells. You can also use it to anoint any candles you're using in love spells.

♥ *Chocolate*

If you don't believe that chocolate is a love potion, just try giving someone an entire pound of Godiva goodies and see how fast his or her attitude changes. Okay, you may not get laid, but you sure will be looked upon much more favorably. What you do with that foot in the door is up to you.

Another thing to keep in mind is that some people are allergic to chocolate. Never give anyone anything to eat unless you ask first!

Here's a quickie spell for giving a gift of chocolate.

- Buy the chocolates, and none of the el cheapo chocolates, either. Better to have a little of the good stuff than a lot of the artificial junk that tastes like brown erasers. Wrap the box in the most gorgeous paper and ribbon you can find.
- Charge the chocolates with this spell:

May the giving of these chocolates, dark and sweet, draw magic into me that enhances my attractiveness and my romantic qualities. (Okay, it's not so poetic, but it does the job.)

- Then, feeling like Casanova or Helen of Troy, present the chocolates to your intended true love, preferably at a time when the two of you are alone. You'll get asked to share— make the most of the opportunity to show how charming, caring, and thoughtful you can be. If you're *not* asked to share, what on earth do you want with such a rude, selfish person?

♥ Hot Aphrodisiac Chocolate

Again, you're going to want to use good chocolate for this one. Make hot chocolate in the usual way, but add a dash of the following magical spices:

Cinnamon, charged for male sexual energy (a cinnamon stick stirred around in the mug is a nice touch. It may be a little phallic, but this *is* a love potion!)
Nutmeg, charged for female sexual energy

As you're stirring all this, and the chocolate is melting into the milk, say this incantation:

*Cinnamon for the passions of man, nutmeg for the passions of woman:
as you come together in this magical potion, so will my love and I
come together in love and desire. This spell is done with harm to none.*

This is actually a great spell for two lovers to do together, he
adding the cinnamon and chanting the appropriate line, she
adding the nutmeg.

Pour the chocolate in two mugs, and take the first sip from
each other's cup.

♥ *Lust-After-Dinner Incense*

This incense has about a two-hour time delay. In other words,
you can do the spell, burn the incense, go out to a romantic
dinner or a movie, then come home and *WOOOO-HOOOO!*

You have your choice here. All these ingredients can be either
powdered *or* chopped into tiny pieces, but make sure that
they're the same. If one is powdered, then all of them should be
powdered. This is so that everything burns evenly.

Thanks for this recipe and the following one to the Witches
of the Temple of Diana. Several of the couples in the temple
tried and tested these concoctions, reporting more than satisfac-
tory results, although the guys advise that you be home when
the time delay factor kicks in, avoiding a long and embarrassing
walk across a crowded restaurant.

Ingredients:

Red sandalwood as a base, two tablespoons
1 teaspoon bergamot
1 teaspoon damiana
1 teaspoon galangal
1 teaspoon orris root
3 drops each ambergris, musk, and civet oils

Charge the ingredients for the following magical properties:

Sandalwood, for honesty
Bergamot, for sensuality
Damiana, also for sensuality
Galangal, for love and magic power
Orris, for love
Ambergris, for virility, sensuality, and passion
Musk, for strength and passion
Civet, for sensuality, passion, and love

♥ *Passion of Africa Incense*

The powerful magic of this incense comes from yohimbe, the bark of an African tree. This is a dark, woody scent, perhaps too strong for some tastes, but a powerhouse aphrodisiac incense. If you'd like to add a touch of sweetness to it, include one or more of the optional oils.

1 or 2 teaspoons powdered or ground yohimbe
1 or 2 teaspoons powdered or ground sandalwood
1 teaspoon frankincense
10 drops musk oil
10 drops jasmine oil
3 drops frangipani oil (optional)
    or 3 drops ylang-ylang oil (optional)

Charge the ingredients for the following magical properties:

Yohimbe, for power and passion
Sandalwood, for honesty
Frankincense, for magical transformation
Musk oil, for passion
Jasmine oil, for happiness
Frangipani oil, for love and sensuality
Ylang-ylang oil, for love

♥ *Lust Incense*

1 teaspoon yohimbe
1 teaspoon damiana
1 teaspoon patchouli
½ teaspoon each cloves, dragon's blood resin, oak moss

Charge all this stuff for the same thing: unbridled, clothes-rippin' lust between lovers.

This incense is courtesy of the Sisterhood of Thalia coven, and making it is one of the few serious magical works that the Sisters perform. The Sisters are devotees of Thalia, the Muse of Comedy, and believe that life is too short not to have fun, and that religion should encompass joy and laughter. However light-hearted the Sisters may be, there's nothing funny at all about this incense. Talk about *hot!* This must be the "joy" part of the Sisters' philosophy.

♥ *Wormwood/Absinthe*

Wormwood (artemisia absinthium) is another herb with legendary aphrodisiacal qualities, but the reputation of wormwood comes mainly from its association with absinthe.

Absinthe is a liqueur made from a distillation of wormwood; this legendary, pale green concoction is both highly addictive and highly dangerous. And highly illegal in this country. I'd advise against trying absinthe as an aphrodisiac, since nothing breaks the romantic mood like a surprise visit from the DEA. And since wormwood and absinthe can be poison, its use is limited unless you happen to be into cold ones, ya pervert.

On the other hand, wormwood burned as an incense has a great reputation for being able to summon spirits, who will then answer your questions. But I'll be honest with you: Unless you're experienced in dealing with spirits, you probably don't want to get into this particular area. Calling spirits is easy. Getting rid of them again can be somewhat trickier.

Wormwood is an antique charm to bring a lover. Put a little red bag of it under the bed while reciting this spell:

> *Magic of wormwood I summon thee,*
> *Bring the perfect lover to me!*

Just to end this chapter with an interesting sidelight, one of the books I used for researching the antique recipes in this book, a work dated 1877, noted that one of the better known and widely used sexual stimulants of the time was flagellation. But if you think I'm getting into details on the whips 'n' chains techniques, you're so, *so* wrong.

The powdered partridge brains were punishment enough.

3

Pagan Love Secrets of the Gods

As private parts to the gods are we: they play with us
for their sport
—Curtis and Elton, *BlackAdder*

The comforting thing about gods and goddesses, especially the gods of Greece and Rome, is that they're a lot like us. They have love problems, marital squabbles, in-law troubles, two-timin' men, and good-time girls. So when you invoke the power of a god to help you out of your love troubles, you're bound to find at least one, and probably several, gods who know *just* what you're talking about. Don't fool around with those little sweetness-and-white-light angels that are the darlings of the New Age set: they don't even have genitalia, so what do they know from sex?

Got a man who runs around? Call on Juno: there are endless stories of her husband Jupiter seducing nymphs, other goddesses, and comely mortals. There's no goddess more willing to help you when you're doing spells to make him keep it in his pants.

Got low self-esteem? Call on Narcissus, the man who *knows* he's too sexy for his shirt. Ask him for his secrets of self-love.

Ready to ditch the controlling boyfriend or girlfriend? Lilith and Diana, the original feminists, are ready to support you and give you the self-confidence you need to do without that loser.

This chapter will take a closer look at the gods of the classical world, the areas of human emotion they represent, and how you can draw on the power of these gods to speed your spells. Remember: Gods are the anthropomorphic forms that we've given to energies, emotions, hopes and fears, and all human traits from the abysmal to the exalted. When you call on a particular god, you're actually calling on the cosmic energies that he/she represents, and it is this particular aspect of natural law that gives the potency to your spellwork.

♥ Aphrodite's Beauty Oil

Mythology is full of stories about nymphs and mortals who wanted to be as beautiful as the goddess of Love and Beauty, and some real airheads who insisted that they were at least as beautiful as, if not more than, Aphrodite.

This was never a good idea in ancient times. Women who bragged about their beauty were just begging to get turned into rocks and flowers and even crawly critters or outright monsters by the jealous goddess. And she was right to do it: people who brag about their great beauty are people who are a pain in the posterior. Aphrodite was just safeguarding the gene pool; these people may have been good-looking, but they had I.Q.s in the negative numbers.

One thing Aphrodite was generous about, however, was *sharing* her beauty, especially with people who also wanted beauty of the spirit.

This oil makes a pretty perfume and a nice incense to use in Scented Fire or in Scent Jars when you do Love Spells. It's also good simmered in water to perfume the room.

You can also use this oil to anoint candles, stones, spells on paper, and other elements of various Love Spells: it gives the spell additional power.

1 dram almond oil as a base
10 drops geranium oil

10 drops lilac oil
10 drops apple oil
1 pinch strawberry leaves
2 pinches catnip
1 amber chip

Mix all ingredients on a Friday closest to the full moon. Empower the oil by chanting seven times:

Aphrodite, born of sea
Grant a boon from you to me
As lovely scent now fills the air
I ask of you, your beauty share.

Hades and Persephone:
Overcoming Parental Disapproval of Your Mate

In the story of Hades and Persephone we have the classic situation of the bride's mother firmly convinced that the groom is not nearly good enough for her little princess. I don't know what Demeter's problem was: Hades was a god, ruler of a kingdom big enough to include five rivers, and he owned all the mineral rights, including the diamond mines. He even had a dog, so you know he loved animals. Not only was he rich, he was tall, dark, handsome, and gloomy: the perfect Gothic romance novel hero.

But Demeter just couldn't see her little girl married to Hades. To her, the Underworld was just another bad neighborhood. So, even though Zeus had promised Hades Persephone's hand in marriage, Demeter kept putting off the wedding and the caterer was getting mighty impatient. And Persephone could hear that old biological clock ticking away.

So the semihappy couple eloped, but things just went from bad to worse, until Persephone agreed to go home to her mother for six months out of the year while Hades took cold showers, tossed back a few brewskis, and called 900 numbers.

Do *not* let this happen to you. If you're having in-law trouble, there are no gods on Olympus more understanding of your problems than Hades and Persephone. Haul out a couple of pomegranates and get yourself some heavy-duty help from the Gods Who've Been There.

♥ *Persephone's Spell to Get the Wedding Date Set*

If Demeter hadn't kept postponing the wedding, Hades wouldn't have had to take matters into his own hands and it would have avoided lots of problems later.

If you and your beloved find that your wedding plans seem to be stalled, or problems come up every time you try to set a date, here's a spell to get things moving again! Be advised: This spell is not a spell to get a mate. You already have to have an agreement to marry. If you're trying to force someone to set a date and he or she keeps putting it off, you might ask yourself exactly why this person is so reluctant. Why would you want to settle for someone who doesn't love you enough to get off his or her butt and down the aisle?

You'll need:

About a foot of white ribbon, wide enough to write on
Two gold rings (fake wedding rings from the dime store are
    fine—it's the symbolism you're after)

Write on the ribbon:

The wedding of [your name and his] *will be held by mutual consent on* [whatever date you want—pick a realistic one, not "tomorrow"], *with no interference and no problems. This spell is done with harm to none.*

Charge one of the rings for you and one for the intended spouse. Slip the rings on the ribbon and tie the ends of the ribbon together to make a circle. If you've got stuff you've been saving to use until after you're married, stash this charm with the rest of it. Otherwise, keep it someplace personal, like your underwear drawer.

♥ Persephone's Violets: A Spell for Peace With the In-Laws

This is a spell that the two of you can do together. Try to remember that peace is achieved when both sides listen a lot and give a little. The Violet Spell is as much for you as for the in-laws or family. Remember also that you're not looking to *win*: This is definitely not a win-lose thing, because when you're not getting along with the people you love, *nobody's* winning. You're looking for peace, harmony, and respect for yourselves as well as for your in-laws.

If you're really having trouble, you might also look at the Athena's Talisman spell, and see if it applies to you.

You'll need:

A potted violet plant. Violets, as well as roses, are sacred to Venus, and the Greeks wore the flowers to cool hot tempers.
Lavender-colored candle, to promote peace
Several small amethyst crystals, the stones of peace
Lavender, charged for peace and harmony, to be burned as incense

Light the charcoal, and while it's getting hot, close your eyes and take several deep breaths. Each time, let your breath out slowly and relax.

You'll be charging the magical tools as you use them. If two of you are doing this spell together, one of you holds the tool, such as the candle, and the other places his or her hands on top of the other's hands. This not only combines your powers, it confirms your bond with each other as the primary force in your lives, that no one else is as important to you or deserves as much care and consideration as the person you love. You made a vow of love with this person, and he or she comes first, forsaking all others.

When the charcoal is ready, spoon on the lavender as incense and let it smolder. Say the incantation:

We offer this incense to great Hades and his Queen, Persephone. We ask your aid and your power in this spell to bring peace and harmony into our home, peace and harmony between us and [names of in-laws]. Let attitudes change, let old grudges be dissolved, let there be open-mindedness on both sides, and let a new spirit of harmony, love, and respect prevail.

Charge the candle with this incantation:

We offer this candle to the spirits of Concord and Peace, that peace and harmony will govern our relationship with [names of in-laws].

Charge the amethysts:

Stones of peace and harmony, bring peace and harmony with [names of in-laws].

Now place the amethysts in a ring around the candle, saying:

As this ring has no beginning and no end, let it draw a circle of peace and harmony around us and [names of in-laws]. No discord can enter in, no serious arguments, no disharmony.

Now, pass the violet plant through the smoke of the lavender incense, to infuse it with the power of the spell, saying:

This violet plant, a symbol of peace and harmony, brings peace between ourselves and [names of in-laws]. This spell is done with harm to none.

Set the violet plant near the candle while the candle burns. After the candle has burned halfway down, put it out and set one of the amethysts in the plant's soil.

Give the plant to the in-laws as a peace offering, completing the circle of peace. Next time they come over, light the remainder of the candle as a reminder of your wishes for harmony.

Lovers United Against Adversity: Athena's Spell and Talisman

In this spell, you'll be making a wax talisman for the united strength of your love, which will help you prevail against obstacles. Hang this talisman somewhere in your house, so that when you see it, you're reminded of your commitment to each other, first and foremost.

Athena was the Greek Goddess of Wisdom. You'll often see Athena in battle armor, since she was also a warrior goddess, but one whose wise judgments could also bring an end to war. Athena knew when to charge forward and when to hold back, and wise generals invoked Athena as well as Ares, the God of War. Good thinking and cool heads can win more battles than naked aggression and hot tempers.

Funny thing about Athena. She was thought to be the personification of two deities: Athena and Pallas, a phallic god of whom very little is known. This means that Pallas Athene, her proper name, is actually female and male, united in strength and wisdom. It also accounts for her symbol: the female symbol topped by a phallic triangle.

If you're doing this spell as part of the spell for Peace With the In-laws you're going to have to ask yourself if you're really ready to let go of being Mommy's and Daddy's little prince or princess. You're two grown-up married people: The time for letting your parents make the rules ended when you signed that marriage certificate and left home. So no matter whose parents they are, you're *both* going to have to lay down the law and support each other.

But that doesn't mean that you have to provoke an argument with the in-laws. That's not going to solve anything, it'll only make things worse. Instead, do the Violet Spell, then the following spell for strengthening your commitment to each other and to your union.

You'll need:

Two Tarot cards: the Lovers and Strength
A 6-inch length of ribbon or string, any color. This will be
    used for hanging the talisman
Two candles: red for courage and strength, yellow or gold for
    a faithful union and success through courage. Votives
    aren't as good for this spell as old-fashioned taper candles
    in candlesticks
A piece of wax paper, aluminum foil, or plastic wrap, set on
    a heatproof surface
Something sharp, like a pencil point, to scratch the design
    into the talisman

Technique for making a wax talisman: You're going to let melted wax drip onto the wax paper (or whatever you're using) to make the talisman. Form the ribbon or string into a loop for hanging, and drip the wax over part of the string, so that it sticks to it. This way, you don't have to make a hole in the talisman later. The technique is to drip a little wax onto the paper, press the two loose ends of the string into it (you can use the pencil to push it into the wax), let it cool a little, then continue doing the spell and dripping the wax. So put the wax paper on a glass plate or a potholder or trivet or something flat and heatproof. You'll peel off the finished talisman when the wax is cool.

The two of you do this spell together. Gather all your materials together on a table, and sit together.

One of you lights the red candle, saying:

We light this candle for the courage and strength of our love, which overcomes all obstacles.

The other lights the yellow candle, saying:

We light this candle for success, that through our faith in each other,
and in our union, we gain strength to overcome all obstacles.

One of you holds the Strength Tarot card, the other holds the
Lovers. Each one of you must tell the other what the card you're
holding means to you, in terms of your relationship. Then,
switch cards and do the same thing.

Place the cards on the table, between the candles, where they
will remind you of the strength of love as you make the talisman.

Drip wax onto the wax paper and stick the ribbon or string
into it. Then say the following incantation:

Great Athena, you who unites male and female energies into one,
give us wisdom, good judgment, united strength, and success. By your
power, we will prevail over those who would interfere with us, not by
battle or harsh words, but by good judgment, wise decisions, and soft
but firm words. Through our united strength, let us make peace with
ourselves and others. This spell is done with harm to none.

Now start dripping wax from the two candles onto the wax
paper. You should have fun with this! Let the colors blend and
run together: this is the sign of your unity. When you've got
enough wax built up and the wax has firmed up a little, but not
cooled, inscribe Athena's symbol into the wax, and both your

first names. Let the wax cool thoroughly, then peel the talisman
off the paper. If you have trouble getting the talisman free, just
leave the paper attached and trim the paper around the edges.
Hang the talisman in your home.

♥ *Lilith's Spell to Banish a Controlling Lover*

Long before the advent of Christianity, Lilith was a Sumerian/
Babylonian earth goddess called Belili, the Divine Lady. Her

symbol was the lily. The goddess Astarte, Goddess of Creation, was also called Lilith.

The Hebrews turned the Divine Lady into an object lesson, so that women wouldn't remember their power and threaten the patriarchy.

In the Hebrew story, Lilith and Adam, the first woman and man, were created equal. One day Adam suggested that the two of them get together and . . . you know, nudge nudge, wink wink.

"Sounds great to me," said Lilith, "And to make it interesting, I'll even get on top."

"But wait a minute," Adam said. "You have to get on the bottom, because you're supposed to be beneath me and subservient to me in all things. You're the frailer sex, ya know."

Lilith burst into unbelieving laughter. "Get *back,*" she told Adam. "That's way too high a price to pay for a little boinking, babe. C'mere. . . . lemme tell ya what you can do with your missionary position."

And she suggested an alternate position, which would have to wait until either there was another guy in the Garden of Eden, or until the invention of the strap-on marital aid.

According to the old story, Lilith took off, to live alone by the Red Sea and to take as many lovers as she pleased—none of whom, presumably, minded the woman getting on top.

To discredit Lilith, the patriarchs declared her a demon, a succubus, a killer of children. This is to teach women what happens when you disobey a husband's commands. Or what happens if you have the colossal nerve to actually *enjoy* getting laid, you hussy.

Modern women have given Lilith back her stolen divinity and honor her as the first feminist. Along with Diana, the virgin Goddess of the Moon, Lilith is the patroness of independent women.

In the spirit of equality, however, Lilith is willing to help anyone, female or male, who is being dominated by a lover or spouse.

This is a two-part spell: The first part of this spell, Lilith's, breaks the control of the person and binds the controlling actions.

The second part, Diana's, strengthens the independence of the person doing the spell, so you can let go and start over without the controlling person.

Do this spell just before the dark moon, when the light is dwindling. This is the best time for getting things out of your life.

You're going to have to be in the right frame of mind for this. You have to *want* to get out from under someone's domination. Many people have submissive personalities, and they cry about how they're given no freedom by their mates or lovers, and they're tired of being told what to do and being criticized, yet they feel that this very domination "proves" that the lover "really loves" them. All it proves is that the dominator needs a willing victim to make himself or herself feel superior. Without that victim, they're nothing. Secure, self-confident people don't need to be either victim or persecutor.

No spell is going to magically make this person just go away. You're going to have to confront this person and end the relationship in no uncertain terms. But remember—this is a spell for a "controlling" lover, *not* an abusive one. *To get rid of an abuser, you should get the help and advice of professionals, like the police and a social services person, and make sure you're not in danger.*

But if you want to get rid of someone who just can't seem to stop telling you what to do, or keeps finding fault with you, do this spell to help you through the breakup process. And you know what? You don't even need to argue with this person. All you really have to say is "It isn't working for me, I don't want to see you anymore." Nobody can argue with that or tell you that you're wrong about what you choose.

A controller will want to get you in an argument to make you explain your decision: A controller knows that being put on the defensive is the best way to break your confidence and get you to back down. The longer the argument drags on, the better it is for the controller. If you feel that you have to offer a logical explanation or defend yourself against the controller's bogus charges, you're lost. You don't have to explain yourself to this person: Who does she think she is? Your mother? Most people look upon any kind of confrontation as though they're in a court of law and have to prove they're right. But you don't have to prove a thing. Just stick to your guns and walk off. If the controller has no one to argue with, he or she can't win. The only explanation you have to give—*and you're not required to give any reason at all*—is "Because I don't *want* to." You're not required to be logical when it comes to what you want in life—or what you want to get out of your life!

You'll need:

- A lily, in Lilith's honor
- An old light bulb
- A piece of paper on which to write your spell
- Someplace safe to smash the light bulb. A good way to do it is put the light bulb inside a couple of plastic grocery bags and break it inside the bags. Less glass to clean up, same effect.
- A black candle
- A small bottle or jar with a lid, an old one, not a pretty or decorative one
- Black string or thread (if you don't have black, plain string will do. I like to use black crochet thread for binding spells)
- Pen with black ink
- Incense: frankincense and myrrh, charged for banishing bad influences and bad energy from your life, for cleansing and purifying energy

Close your eyes and take a few deep breaths to relax. Hold the lily between your hands and say:

Lilith, Creator Goddess and woman complete in yourself, I invoke your aid and offer you this lily as my thanks. Give me the power as I banish [name of controller] *from my life, to keep* [his/her] *actions, thoughts or words from having any power or effect on me. This spell is done with harm to none.*

Lay the lily on the ground, if you're outside, or place it in a vase if you're inside. When it finally fades and withers, don't just throw it out; take it outside and leave it on the ground.

Light the charcoal and spoon on the incense.

On the paper write the following spell, then read it aloud:

By the power of the Goddess Lilith, I banish [name of controller] from my life. I banish [his/her] power over me. I bind and banish all [his/her] thoughts, words, intents or actions that might affect me. I bind and banish all my love and affection for [him/her], and my conscious or unconscious need to be with this person or controlled by [him/her]. This person is nothing to me now and has no more effect on me. I have no more interest in anything [he/she] says or does. I separate myself from this person. This spell is done with harm to none.

Pass the paper through the smoke of the incense. As you do that, say:

This sacred smoke cleanses and purifies my life.

Roll or fold the paper up tightly, to a size that will fit in the jar. Then wrap the paper with the black thread or string. Use as much as you feel you need. Light the black candle and drip wax on the string—again, as much as you feel you need.

Put the paper into the bottle or jar, but don't screw the lid on yet.

Take the light bulb in your hands and say:

This is the end of this controlling relationship. I am finished with it.

Making sure you don't cut yourself, break the light bulb. Really give it a good smash and feel your connection with this controlling person ending. As you do it, say,:

[name], I break your hold over me!

Very carefully (we don't use blood in spells!), pick out some of the glass and put it in the bottle or jar with the spell.

Now screw on the lid. Drip black wax along the edges of the jar lid to magically seal the jar, closing in the actions of the controlling person.

Then bury the jar. If it's winter and the ground is frozen, or you can't conveniently bury it, then hide it in a place where you're pretty certain it will never be found.

Sit quietly by yourself for a little while after you do this spell and think about what needs to come next. Just making the decision to get out of the relationship should make you feel a lot stronger.

♥ *Diana's Spell to Regain Your Independence*

Do this spell right after you do Lilith's spell. You'll need:

A white votive candle
Small rose quartz crystals, for self-confidence
A nice moonstone or clear quartz crystal, charged for Diana
    and independence. You'll carry or wear this afterward as a
    talisman
Incense: oak or pine, charged for strength

For more information on Diana, see Diana's Spell for Virgins later in this chapter. Diana is the Moon Goddess, an independent woman living on her own terms. She rules the moon and the tides, she is the source of dreams and intuition. Obviously, Diana is very big with feminists, but she is actually a source of strength for all women, whatever their political leanings. If you're a man and doing this spell, you might want to substitute Apollo the Sun God for his sister, Diana. (See the following Apollo's Spell.) The changes for the invocation are in parentheses.

Light your charcoal and start your incense smoldering. As you add the incense on the charcoal, say:

*I charge this incense for strength of my decisions and my will, and offer
it to you, Great Diana [or Great Apollo], as my thanks for your help.*

Light the candle and place the rose quartz crystals in a ring
around it. As you place the stones, see them not as small stones,
but as boulders—great stones representing the strength and
good judgment you need to make your own decisions in life, independent of anyone else's approval. These stones may be small,
but they're still rock, as firm as mountains, and have retained
their strength through centuries.

Pass the moonstone or quartz crystal through the smoke of
the incense to infuse the stone with the strength of the Goddess,
then hold the stone in your hands and say this spell:

*Great Diana [or Great Apollo], I invoke your aid in strengthening
me with independence, clear thinking, and the ability to make wise
decisions on my own. Give me a new sense of responsibility for
myself, and the courage to claim and defend my independence.
Infuse this crystal with your power, as my reminder that I share that
power and independence with you.*

Let the candle burn for a while, while you sit quietly and listen to any thoughts or ideas the Goddess or God sends you to
strengthen you.

❤ Apollo's Spell for Male Independence

This is essentially the same spell, done with a male emphasis.
Diana's brother is Apollo, the Sun God. Together they represent
the balance of male and female energy, which is necessary to generate life. If you're a man doing this spell, you might feel more
comfortable invoking Apollo's aid instead of Diana's, although
Witches believe that we all contain a balance of male and female
energy, so you can invoke either Goddess or God and the spell
will still work for you. If you're working with Apollo, make the
following substitutions to Diana's Spell:

A yellow or gold candle, charged for the Sun God
Sunstones, golden topaz, citrine, or tiger's eye for Apollo

Good-Hearted Women in Love
With Two-Timin' Men
(and vice-versa)

One thing you have to say about Hades: When he finally got married, he was faithful. You never hear stories about Hades hot-footing it around flashy young nymphs when Persephone's visiting her mother.

On the other hand, his brother Jupiter, the chief god of Olympus, simply could not keep his hands to himself. There are hundreds of stories about Jupiter's seducing nymphs, other goddesses, and mortal women—who usually got turned into stones, flowers, birds, or whatever by Jupiter's wife, Juno. This guy got more unauthorized nookie than a member of the U.S. Congress. When her husband wasn't home, at least Juno knew where he was: with another woman. This gets rather wearying with time.

So, how do you do a spell to keep a man home and stop him from running around?

Honey, you don't.

If you have to use magic to keep this guy at home, you're gonna have to ask yourself exactly how much he loves you. Besides, using magic to force someone to do something is black magic.

Instead, why don't you do Juno's Spell? You do this one to ask yourself exactly how much you're willing to take, how many times you're going to be humiliated before you realize that although he may be the Only One for you, you're Only One Among Many for him.

And guys, if you have a two-timin' woman, Juno is perfectly willing to help you, too. Misery loves company.

❤   *Juno's Keep It In His Pants Spell*

This one's real easy. You need:

A piece of paper with that no-good, scum-suckin', two-timer
  runaround's name on it
An ice cube
A heatproof bowl
A microwave or a regular oven. If your oven has a door,
  great. If not, keep it slightly open and keep peeking in.

Put the paper in the bottom of the bowl. Put the ice cube on
top of the paper. Stick the bowl in the microwave oven. Or the
regular oven.

As the ice melts all over that snake, say this spell:

*Great Juno, Queen of the Gods, as this ice turns to water, let this
person's infidelity cease to hurt me. I take away his/her power to
hurt me anymore, to make me feel unloved and unhappy. My love
and my heartache melt away like this ice. This spell is done with
harm to none, even no harm to that lowlife jerk.*

Then throw the water down the toilet and throw the paper
into the trashcan with the rest of the garbage.

You might also want to check the chapter on Anti-Love Spells
if you want to get rid of this cut-rate Casanova.

❤   *Juno's Intertwined Roses Spell*

Juno is the Goddess of Marriage, although she had a real hard
time of it married to Jupiter. However, she stuck by him, and it
was Juno he loved above all.

This is a nice spell to do as part of a handfasting or wedding
ceremony, or when the two of you decide to make a commitment
to your love. You twine the roses together and bind your fates together with nine knots and nine wishes. In this case, it's good to
have roses with thorns! This should be done by the two of you.

You'll need:

A long-stemmed red rose, charged for male energies
A long-stemmed white rose, charged for female energies
Nine short lengths of yellow ribbon, charged for the energy
  of the sun and for happiness

Start by stripping off the thorns. Every time you eliminate a thorn, visualize overcoming and eliminating all "thorny" elements or obstacles to your love.

Then twine the stems of the two roses together. As you do this, visualize your love for each other, the entwining of your lives. Use the yellow ribbons and tie nine knots evenly spaced down the length of the stems, at each knot make a wish for your happiness and your hopes for your future together.

Hang the entwined roses in the home you make together.

Vesta's Sacred Fire

Vesta is the Roman Goddess of the Hearth and Home. A sacred fire was kept burning in her temple in the heart of Rome, tended by six Vestal Virgins. This fire was supposedly brought to Rome from the ruins of Troy by the hero Aeneas, and the perpetual flame was thought to be essential to the security of civic and family life in Rome. If the fire ever went out, Rome's fortunes would suffer.

Also central to the Roman family were the *lares*, household spirits of the family. These spirits were honored with a small altar, the *lararium*, set up in an honored place in every Roman house. Quite often, the lararium was decorated with vases of fresh flowers.

As Rome was the center of the world, your home is the center of your family. Let Vesta's sacred fire bring warmth, love, and security to everyone who lives there, including the guardian spirits of your house and family. This spell is a very simple ritual, setting up a small lararium in your home, and honoring your ancestors as guardian spirits. This is to remind you and your family of the importance of each other's love, that even those relatives no longer in this world are still loved and loving members of the family.

You'll need:

Several small photos of your immediate family and ancestors: parents, grandparents, or other close relatives, living or dead

A yellow or gold votive candle, or a plain votive candle in a yellow or gold holder (gold and yellow are sun colors, the colors of ongoing life and strength, in this case, the strength and life of the family)

Fresh flowers in a vase or potted plants (optional, but nice)

Gather your family pictures together on a table or shelf. As you set up the pictures, recall something wonderful and loving about each family member, both the living and the dead. Every member of the family is important: all these people are connected, all of them make up who and what you are.

Set the pictures up, and set the votive candle in front of the group of pictures, but don't light it yet. You'll do that after you say the spell:

By the Goddess Vesta, who protects and guards the home and family, I empower this candle for the ongoing life of this family. I light this candle to honor you, and to honor our family, the living and the dead, and invoke your aid and the aid of our guardian spirits in keeping us strong, in happiness and love, through times of trouble and times of joy.

Then light your candle. You don't have to keep it burning constantly, as the Vestal Virgins did, but this is a good spell to do once a month, or in times of family crisis or family celebration.

The lararium can be kept in place all the time, and added to as the need arises. If you can get your entire family to join you in this spell, it's even better.

The Gods of Ancient Britain

So far, we've talked about the better-known gods of the Greek and Roman pantheon. But at one time the entire world was Pagan, and each culture, country, town, and even individual clan had its own special gods. With the renewed interest in these older gods, and the growing resurgence of Paganism as a restored religion, we're learning more about them and their worship and how they can help us in everyday life.

Certainly one of the biggest revivals is of the gods of ancient Britain and the gods of the Norse people—rich, varied pantheons with gods who are vividly alive.

Jane Raeburn was trained in a Welsh-oriented Wiccan coven. Among the goddesses worshipped in her coven was Rhiannon, a Celtic goddess made famous in the Stevie Nicks song, "Rhiannon." In the ancient myth, Rhiannon was a magical being on a white horse, beautiful and unattainable, who governed love and lust. In Jane's coven, Rhiannon is invoked at the first quarter moon, so time your spell accordingly.

♥ Rhiannon's Spell for Difficult Times

While we visualize Rhiannon as a maiden, young and flirtatious, the rest of her myth concerns much darker matters. When called upon, she can be a powerful helper at those times when love places too great a burden on us.

If you are in such a position, find a time and space where you can be alone and comfortable. Light your space with candles, and put on some Celtic or New Age music (nothing too intrusive). Sit or lie down in a relaxed position and visualize a circle of white light forming to protect you and your space. Have at hand an apple and a glass of white wine or white grape juice.

If you like, you can formally cast the circle by walking around its perimeter holding a wand or sacred knife, or simply inscribing its boundary with your finger, and saying, "Circle of Power, I conjure thee to be a place of safety, where only good may enter."

The next part is your formal meditation. It may help to make an audio tape of this so that you can concentrate on doing it rather than remembering or reading it. Or, if you're able to find another person you can trust to perform this role, you can have someone read it to you as you perform the visualization.

Now relax fully, knowing that this place is truly safe. Feel the connection of your body to the earth and "shed" your earthly problems and concerns by feeling them dissipate down your body and into the ground. Make your mind as blank as possible. When thoughts arise, gently send them into the earth as well.

Now visualize yourself standing in a green field surrounded by trees. It is springtime, and you are surrounded by new life— flowers, birds, fragrances, bursting new leaves. Take a moment to enjoy this place.

From out of the trees come a horse and rider. The horse is white, fresh, lively. The woman is young, beautiful, and her clothing seems to lie lightly on her. She has tumbled red-gold hair and radiant blue eyes. You are drawn to her, and she smiles deliciously but keeps moving, across the field and down a path between two apple trees.

You follow her down the path, which turns and twists between two high hedges filled with singing birds. She remains elusive, just in sight, disappearing around the next curve. You cannot help but laugh, for you know this is part of the essence of the Lady you seek.

Finally you come to a clearing where a big, gnarled, old apple tree rises beside a well. She is nowhere to be seen, yet you do not feel the journey has been worthless. You approach the well and find that you have brought a gift or offering to be made to Rhiannon. Look at it and remember what you give, then drop it into the water, perhaps with a word or two spoken over the well to reflect its value and commend it to the Goddess.

Remain by the well until the ripples of your offering disappear. Suddenly you find that you are weary. You settle yourself beside the apple tree, feeling two of the great roots reach around you like arms.

It is now that Rhiannon returns—still beautiful, but not coquettish. She approaches you seriously, kneels beside you and asks you to tell of your pain. If you can do so, speak the words of your trouble out loud or in a whisper.

She listens carefully to all your feelings, and though she may appear too young to know of such serious things, you know that she understands. Though she may appear too weak to share your burden, nonetheless you can entrust some of it to her. She will help you carry your load until you can resume it; she will stay beside you in time of need.

Remain as long as you like in meditation and communion with the Goddess. When you are ready to return, rise, then thank Rhiannon and bid her farewell. You feel stronger now, ready to do what needs to be done. You walk back down the twisting path to the place between the two apple trees, and back into the field of springtime. Open your eyes when you are ready, and return to the place where you are.

Now take up the apple. Say:

Rhiannon, Great Queen, Youth and Beauty, Love and Lust, I thank you and I do not forget you. Hail Rhiannon!

Take a bite of the apple.
Take up the wine or juice.

Rhiannon, Great Queen, Lady of Springtime, Lady of the Green Earth, I thank you and I do not forget you. Hail Rhiannon!

Take a sip.

Leave the apple and pour the rest of the wine or juice in some outdoor place as an offering to Rhiannon. Within three months, at or near a first-quarter moon, repeat this meditation to remember Rhiannon and thank her for her aid.

Eros and Psyche:
Curing Dissatisfaction in Love

You're in love and everything's been fine up until now, but lately you just aren't sure. Your friends tell you that you could do better. And you love your spouse/lover, but he or she could stand some improvement.

Well, you know what? We could all stand some improvement. But a lot of us can't stop questioning a good thing. We keep picking it apart until it's gone.

Eros, the God of Love, was very taken with Psyche, a mortal woman, and set her up in a beautiful palace where she had everything she wanted and was waited on hand and foot. His only requirement was that she never attempt to see his face. His reason for this was to protect Psyche, since it was thought that to look on the face of a god was fatal. I don't know where this idea came from: I look at Sean Connery and Kevin Sorbo every chance I get, and I'm still here. Anyway, each night Eros came to her and they made dynamite love in the dark and Psyche was one happy woman.

Until her sisters came to visit.

Her sisters told her that, yeah, all this splendor and wealth is very nice, but what about your lover? He could be some monster, some really deformed and ugly geek. If Psyche knew what was good for her, she'd get to the bottom of this, and pronto.

So that night, while Eros was sleeping the sleep of the exhausted lover, Psyche bent over him to get a good look. There he was, the God of Love in all his glory and nekkid to boot.

Psyche got so carried away that she tipped the oil lamp she was holding and some of the hot stuff spilled on Eros and woke him up. He looked at her sadly, realizing that she didn't trust him, and he took off. That's when she realized that she loved Eros, and would have loved him even if he'd been king of the nerds, because he loved her and was good to her. So Psyche went to his mother, Aphrodite, who gave Psyche all these impossible tasks to perform before she got Eros back.

Poor Psyche really suffered for love. She found the love of her life, lost him through her own fear and mistrust, then had to go through humiliation and hardship to get him back. When she finally reunited with him, she wasn't the woman she had been: She was much wiser and stronger. She was ready to accept love without questioning it.

This is a Fire Spell, so the usual precautions outlined in chapter 1 apply.

♥ Psyche's Fire

If you're constantly picking at your lover, finding fault and dissatisfied with everything you think that he or she is doing wrong, or could be doing better, maybe it's time you took a hard look at the relationship—or took a hard look at yourself. If this person is so terrible, then why are you together? Did you go into the relationship thinking that you could change him or her to fit the way you think a lover should be? If so, then why did you settle for him or her? Why are you making life miserable for both of you? Why do you assume that your way is the best way? Sometimes people grow apart, or sometimes one partner is ready to move on, but instead of facing that fact, the one who's ready to leave spends a lot of time justifying leaving, "demonizing" the partner so that you have a "valid excuse" to go. The real question is: Do you still love this person?

Meanwhile, why make someone else unhappy? Psyche's Fire is a clarifying spell that lets you look at the relationship, at your lover, and at yourself. If you find that you need to begin the process of being more considerate to your lover, this is a good spell to do more than once.

You'll need:

The equipment for Scented Fire Spells, as in chapter 1
Frankincense and myrrh resins or oils to burn in the fire.
   Charge the frankincense and myrrh for truth and for
   purification and cleansing.

While making your fire, and before you add the alcohol, place a few lumps of frankincense and myrrh resins in equal amounts in the fire container or, if you're using oils, eight to ten drops of each. Then add the alcohol and light your fire.

As the fire burns, say

Spirit of Psyche, teach me your lessons. Help me to see my lover and myself in true light. Help me free myself of false expectations, and see the relationship as it really is. If the fault is mine, let me see it. Help me be kinder to my lover and more accepting.

Watch the fire as it burns. When it goes out, close your eyes and listen to any answers that just pop into your head. You may not get all the answers—you may even get more questions to ask yourself. If that happens, do the entire spell again another night, and concentrate on the new questions. What you're look-ing for here is to end your dissatisfaction, and if that means reevaluating what you expect from a lover, then you ask your-self if you're willing to let go of old ideas.

Love and Gullibility

Procris was just about the stupidest woman in all of ancient mythology. And there's no record of whether or not she was even a blonde.

She was married to Cephalus, a hunter. Every day, Cephalus would go out in the woods with his spear. By noontime

Cephalus was hot, tired, and sweaty. So he'd take a little break. He'd lie down and talk to the summer breeze (okay, so we won't question his sanity, just go with the story here), saying, "Come sweet Breeze and fan me. You know I love you." Well, a friend of his happened to be passing by and overheard this and told Procris that her hubby was meeting some tart in the woods for a little nooner when he was supposed to be working. Procris wanted to hear for herself, so she sneaked out there and listened. She couldn't see anything, but she heard Cephalus say, "Sweet Breeze, I love you." He was running on about the beautiful breeze when he thought he heard a rustling in the bushes. Thinking it was dinner, he hurled his spear in that general direction. When he rushed over to see what he'd killed, he found Procris mortally wounded. Her last words were: "Oh, Cephalus, when I'm dead, just promise me you won't marry that Breeze!"

Procris may have had all the brains of a gallon of garden mulch, but it's true that nasty gossip can make even the smartest of us doubt ourselves and our love. What's needed is a hard-working charm to stop gossip, and the wisdom to stop paying attention to everything we hear.

For this charm, we'll invoke the powers of Venus, who not only brings love but who protects it.

♥ Venus Anti-Gossip Charm

This is actually a pomander ball, a dried orange stuck with cloves that you can hang up in a closet or a small room to provide a sweet, spicy scent. (The pomander ball was very popular with the Victorians.)

You'll need:

1 small orange or tangerine
A jar of whole cloves, not powdered
Powdered orris root, sacred to Venus

About 18 inches of red ribbon and nine straight pins
Charcoal for incense burning

Lay out the ribbon, and set the orange or tangerine upright on it at the midpoint. You're going to use the ribbon as a hanging loop for the orange. Stick a straight pin through the ribbon, into the bottom of the orange. Bring the ribbon up both sides of the orange, sticking three pins evenly spaced in each side. Tie a knot in the top of the ribbon, and stick two straight pins through the knot, angling them a little to each side. Then make a loop to hang the orange by tying the ends together.

Charge the orange for truth and the cloves to stop gossip. Make a few small cuts in the orange with a sharp knife, not deep, just enough to prick the skin. Stick the whole cloves into the orange, covering as much of the surface as possible, but saving a few cloves to burn as incense. Then roll the orange in the orris root. Orris not only adds a nice scent, but has long been associated with ensuring love and driving out evil.

When you're done, light the charcoal and burn the remaining cloves as incense.

Pass the charm through the smoke and repeat this incantation:

Great Venus, I offer you this charm of orange and orris in your honor. I invoke your aid to stop gossip about me or my lover, and to give me the wisdom to stop listening to the idle talk of others.

> *As this charm passes through scent of clove*
> *Gossip will cease and our love will grow.*

Hang the charm someplace dark and dry. Be sure to check on it, to make sure the ribbon is still firmly attached and the pins aren't slipping as the orange dries. The orange will dry out eventually, and the fruit, cloves, and orris will give off a sweet scent.

♥   *Aphrodite's Incense and Spell to Heal
Lovers' Misunderstandings*

You'll need:

   Sandalwood base, charged for good luck in love
   Vetiver oil, charged for love, and hex-breaking (if needed)
   Yohimbe, for lust between lovers
   Crumbled rose petals, for healing between lovers

When the charged ingredients are mixed, say this spell to
make the incense more effective:

*Great Aphrodite, I invoke your power to help heal misunderstandings
and disagreements between me and my lover. Help us see both sides
of the problem, and give both of us love's wisdom and understanding,
that we may grow in tolerance for each other's faults. This spell is
done with harm to none.*

Burn this incense when you're talking out a problem between
you. The important thing is getting the dialogue going and
keeping an open mind.

♥   *Narcissus's Reminder for Self-Esteem*

Narcissus was the most beautiful young man in the ancient
world, and—*whoa!*—didn't he know it. He spent all day looking at himself in a pond, admiring his own reflection. If this guy
were here today, he'd definitely be a model for Calvin Klein.

Okay, so he got turned into a flower for being so conceited,
but that's not the point. The point is that a little self-esteem goes
a long way. For more information on the benefits of self-esteem
in love, see chapter 5.

You'll need:

   A potted narcissus *bulb*—not a full-blown plant. Get these at
      any garden store; you can get the bulbs already potted and
      ready to grow, or you can buy just the bulb and plant it

yourself. Either way, if you're not great at green things, ask
somebody at the plant store for instructions on how to
grow it and care for it.

A few small crystals charged for the following purposes: rose
quartz for self-esteem, agate for self-improvement, garnet,
red jasper, or flint for courage

Set the narcissus plant in a sunny spot, a place that feels good
to you, a place where you can have some privacy. Charge the
stones, and either place them in a ring around the flowerpot, or
in a ring in the soil of the plant. Repeat the spell:

*Spirit of Narcissus, I invoke your help in discovering my own special
qualities, my own worth and gaining the courage to banish all
negative thoughts and patterns that would destroy my self-confidence.*

Each day, sit in front of the plant for a few minutes and take
those minutes to concentrate on something good about yourself.
You might even come up with something that needs improvement—but realizing that you have an area that could use some
work is your strength. You can't change it until you know what
it is. However, this spell is for positive thoughts. Don't let the
negative become a habit. For every negative thought that comes
up, find something positive about yourself. As the narcissus
grows, feel yourself grow in confidence and strength of character.

Note: Not all bulbs actually sprout. If you get one that doesn't
grow, it's not a sign from the gods—it's a sign of plant genetics.
Just go get another bulb and do the spell again.

♥ Diana's Love Spell for Virgins

This isn't a spell to *get* a virgin, it's a spell to do if you *are* one.
So, you dirty old men—and dirty old women (this is an equal-
opportunity insult)—can just go on to chapter 6.

Lots of virgins look at sex with overly romantic eyes. When
you haven't done it, it's easy to imagine how it's going to be

the magical moment of your existence, especially if you watch a lot of movies. In the movies, everyone looks great and does it perfectly.

In real life, there are many disappointments.

But not always. So you virgins should take your time and choose wisely. You only do it for the first time once (thank the gods!) and because it's a one-time deal, why not make it as great as possible?

Don't think of it as "losing" your virginity. Think of it as a beautiful gift you're *giving* someone, and make sure that someone is a person who will respect and appreciate it.

Being a woman of experience, kinda like Liz Taylor, naturally I can't resist giving advice, and my advice is: What's your hurry? There are as many good reasons for staying a virgin as there are for not staying one, maybe more.

Among the really stupid reasons for having sex, at the all-time number-one top spot is: "Because everyone else is doing it and I feel like a freak." And running a real, real close second is: "Because my boyfriend/girlfriend is pressuring me." This one really chips my nail polish. I *hate* that!

To both these "reasons," let me give you one answer: Who's running your life? You or somebody else? Who is better qualified than you to make this decision? Who has to live with the aftermath? You'll wake up and realize that what could have been a really wonderful moment for you was spoiled by the knowledge that it was just something you did to get somebody off your back (so to speak). Whoever you give your virginity to should appreciate it for the gift it is, not look at it as something you had to be talked into just so they could get off. If someone is telling you that you either do it or lose him—lose *him*. I mean, *what an insult!* In other words, all he wants is your body. It might be dressed up in fancy words, but that's the bottom line. The old "I love you, so why won't you prove your love for me" line is the creakiest in the book. Don't fall for it. Any love that you have to "prove" isn't love. Love is mutual respect. Does this sound like respect to you?

And while we're at it, this is the age of AIDS. Are you willing to die for love? Because if you throw precaution to the winds, that's exactly what your choice is. The only bareback riders these days, babe, are in the circus.

So those are the negatives. Now, what about the positives?

First, realize that sex and love are not mutually inclusive. One does not necessarily lead to the other. Just because you have sex with someone doesn't mean that you have an obligation to love that person forever. And just because you love someone, it doesn't mean that you have to have sex. What is absolutely necessary is respect. Although, I'll tell you the truth . . . sex is 100 percent better if you're in love.

If you're planning on having sex with someone experienced, then that can work out well, if the person knows you're a virgin and is willing to respect that. If both of you are virgins, that can work out well also, although be prepared for some mistakes. So what? Who said you have to be experts? No matter that sex is supposed to be "natural," technique is still something you can learn with experience. If it weren't, there wouldn't be a billion-dollar market for how-to books on better sex.

If you're a virgin who wants to make sure that his or her first experience is a good one, there's no better goddess to guide you than Diana, the Virgin Goddess of the Moon. Just because she's chaste doesn't mean she doesn't know a few things about love and passion. The old use of the term *virgin* didn't necessarily mean someone who'd never had sex. It meant a woman who wasn't married and could take care of herself. Diana had passionate flings with beautiful boys on more than one occasion, and some of them she didn't even turn into elks or statues or something afterwards. But it took a lot to win Diana: She was a woman who thought for herself, who didn't mind living independently, unmarried and unmated. In other words, she decided

for herself whom she would be with, or whether she would have
sex at all. She made wise choices. Her men certainly respected
her in the morning. Of course, it's important to respect someone who has the power to turn you into a garden slug.

Diana is a triple goddess, that is, she was thought to represent the three ages of woman: the adventurous young maiden;
the mature, understanding mother; and the older crone who has
the wisdom of age. She is one of the most important goddesses
of the Witches, because she can see situations from all aspects.

You'll need:

A moonstone or clear quartz crystal, both are sacred to Diana
A white or silver votive candle, in honor of the Moon
    Goddess
Jasmine oil for incense; charge the jasmine for spiritual love

Light the charcoal and smolder a few drops of jasmine oil
until the sweet scent fills the room.

Light the silver or white candle, saying

*Diana of the Moon, I offer this candle in your honor, and in thanks
for your help.*

Then pass the moonstone or quartz crystal in and out of the
smoke, to infuse it with the vibrations for spiritual love, as well
as physical love. Hold the crystal between your hands and say
this invocation:

*Great Diana, chaste Goddess, whose freedom would not be bound, I
invoke your aid in giving me good judgment in deciding the matter
of my virginity, and your support in standing by my decision. When
I decide the time is right, guide me to a sexual partner who will
respect me and my independence, who will appreciate the gift I have
to give, and who will be careful and considerate. For these purposes,
I empower this crystal as a charm to ward off unworthy lovers, and
to strengthen me in my choices.*

Let the candle burn a while in a safe place.

Love Spells from Legendary Beasts:
The Power of the Dragon

Salem's Clan of the Dragon has been working with the power of these fascinating creatures for several years. Dragons may no longer exist on the physical plane, but the spirits of the great dragons are certainly still with us. Here's a little dragon lore, and a wonderful spell from the Clan. There are two more in other chapters.

Dragons are the most powerful creatures inhabiting the mythical realms. They are symbols of strength, power, wisdom, cunning, wealth, and longevity. In many cultures, they are seen as the embodiment of the power of Nature. By calling on their assistance it is possible to give *any* spell an added boost of power. Dragons can help you to achieve the goals of self-confidence, personal power and strength, independence, prosperity, and happiness.

Before you do any spell using dragon magic, buy a small pewter dragon figurine. Be sure it's a nice one, not one that is comical or evil looking. This shows the dragon spirits that you respect them and appreciate their help. One word of caution: Never *command* a dragon to give its assistance, always ask politely. If you attempt to command them, you will only succeed in insulting them and destroy any possibility of cultivating a powerful magical alliance. Besides, dragons are known for being extremely wise-assed and sarcastic. Insult 'em and you'll never hear the end of it. Remember that they are perfectly capable of looking upon you as an appetizer.

♥ *Dragon Love Talisman*

This spell should be done on a Friday night closest to the full moon and is designed to attract love to you. For this you will need:

    A small thin wooden disk approximately 3 inches in
       diameter
    A small picture of two entwined dragons
    Glue
    Crafter's sealant or clear nail polish
    Love oil or love potion
    Love or patchouli incense
    One pink candle (to attract a woman) or blue candle
       (to attract a man)
    Rose quartz necklace
    Red or pink bag big enough to hold the finished disk

Glue the picture of the dragons to the wooden disk and let dry. Then coat with the clear crafter's sealant or nail polish to protect the picture (this should be done at least a day ahead of time).

On the day you will be doing the spell, prepare yourself first by taking a luxuriant bubble bath, and then fixing yourself up as if you were getting ready to meet the love of your life. When you are done, gather the above items and go to your magical workspace.

Inscribe the candle with the following symbol inside a heart:

Anoint the candle with the love oil or love potion while concentrating on bringing the perfect lover and partner into your life. Place the candle back in its holder and light it. Light the incense if you have not already done so.

Pick up the wooden dragon disk and anoint it with the love oil or love potion (just on the back is fine if you are unsure about smearing the picture). Pass the disk through the incense smoke and over the candle flame while chanting nine times:

Dragon lovers entwined in flight
Bring to me a love that's bright!

Set the dragon disk down in front of the candle and use the necklace to encircle the disk with rose quartz. Repeat the above chant again nine times while visualizing pink energy coming from the rose quartz and being sucked up by the dragon disk. When the energy transfer is complete, leave everything where it is until the candle burns itself out (or burns down to the holder if this is safer).

Take the bag and paint it with the symbol used on the candle, again inside a heart, then place the bag next to the candle. When the candle burning is complete, put the new dragon love talisman inside the bag and keep it there when you are not using it. To activate the talisman, take it out of its bag just before you go out anywhere, and say the dragon lover's chant nine times. Repeat the spell each month on the Friday closest to the full moon until you have met your perfect love.

4

Friendship and Family Spells

A friend is someone who'll help you move. A true friend
is someone who'll help you move a corpse.

—Anonymous quote
from the Internet

When people think of love spells, they don't usually think of friendship as a form of love. But sometimes, the strongest, truest love is between friends. We forgive faults in friends that we'd never forgive in lovers; we forgive our friends even as we hold grudges against family members for years. In our friends, we see reflected the best of us, or see qualities in them that we only wish we had.

We can have friends that we haven't seen for twenty years, but we still consider them our best friends. The history between us is what binds us to them.

Family is different. The most misunderstandings and the most unrelenting feuds are between family members who actually do love each other but just can't get past the emotional roadblocks. Our friends accept us at our best: our families have seen us at our worst.

But, for better or worse, our friends and family make up our lives, they contribute to who and what we are. They influence our thinking, our everyday activities; they leave deep marks on us, and we on them.

Friends may even be more important in our lives than lovers. Lovers come into our lives and can drift out quickly, but it's our friends who help us through the breakups. As Sonia Braga said in *Moon Over Parador,* "Someone to have sex with you can always find. But a friend. . . ?"

These spells are to strengthen the ties between you and your friends and your family, to clear up misunderstandings and long-simmering grudges, to polish away the tarnish, so that the true gold of friendship gleams.

❤ *Thelma and Louise Potion and Perfume*

Girlfriends, why drive your car off a cliff to prove your friendship, when you can just as easily use this recipe? Equal amounts of rose and lavender steeped in water makes a potion to strengthen the bonds of friendship between women. Or use rose and lavender oils in a sweet almond oil base and share it with your friend as a perfume, or use it to anoint candles or tools in magical workings between friends.

If you're a Witch in an all-female coven, this oil is perfect for an anointing oil to use in the religious rites, or sprinkle the potion at the four quarters when you cast the circle. Rose and lavender also make a nice incense.

One dram of sweet almond oil as a base
8 drops of rose oil
3 drops of lavender oil, or adjust the drops until you have
   the balance you like

❤ *Damon and Pythias Potion*

In Sicily, where folk magic still has a firm grip, especially among the descendants of freed Roman slaves, the story of Damon and

Pythias is a model for loyalty between friends. Pythias was condemned to death by Dionysius, the ruler of Syracuse, and asked time to go home and get his affairs in order and say his final good-bye to his family. Damon offered to stay as a hostage until Pythias returned, but Dionysius said that if Pythias didn't return by a specified day and hour, Damon would die in his friend's place.

Pythias meant well, but his return trip was one of those journeys from hell, in which everything goes wrong. Pythias made it back to Syracuse just as Damon's head was lowered onto the executioner's block. "Hold your sword! I'm here!" Pythias cried.

Dionysius was so amazed that Pythias bothered to come back just to save his friend that he pardoned him. Not only that, but Dionysius became a friend to both of them.

This one's for the guys. Equal amounts of oak and pine. You can get oak and pine sawdust from a lumberyard and simmer in a potion or mix the sawdust in equal parts with sandalwood as a base for incense. The same scents can't really be used as a men's fragrance oil, because the pine will make you smell like bathroom cleaner. However, patchouli oil is a wonderful scent for men. So is oak moss, blended with a little vetiver oil. Add the oils gradually to a base of almond oil until you like the scent.

This is a nice anointing oil for all you studly and sensitive Iron Johnnies. (We women love ya, guys! There's nothing sexier than a man who just got back from one of those Men's Weekend gatherings.) Again, if you're a Witch in an all-male coven, use the incense and/or the potion.

♥ Healing Emotional Scars

The term *dysfunctional family* is an overused one these days. Every third person you talk to will say that they came from a *dysfunctional family*. They have some idea of what a *non*-dysfunctional family is: any family but theirs. And they know, because they saw them on TV when they were growing up: the happy kids, the all-wise mom 'n' dad, the problems that were solved in only a half hour every Thursday night. Or they saw them when they visited a friend's family and wondered how come their own family wasn't like that. As if anyone knows for sure what goes on behind closed doors.

Everyone thinks that everyone else's family is happier than theirs. It's that old "grass is always greener" deal.

Real families are composed of real people, complete with frailties. Human insecurities, doubts, and fears do not simply vanish with the advent of parenthood. The people in our families may not be perfect, but that doesn't mean they are "dysfunctional." Ask any social worker what a *real* dysfunctional family is, and you might see that yours isn't so bad. Social workers work with true horror stories every day.

That doesn't mean that you aren't carrying around some problem left over from childhood. In fact, most of us do. But to hang on to it when you're an adult and capable of charting your own course is futile. The tough thing is to look back not in anger, but in release.

The following *Spell to Ease a Family Quarrel,* another of Kerowyn Silverdrake's beautiful Rune Spells, can be used not only to calm current family disputes, but to release old angers that you could be holding on to from the past or childhood, even anger against a deceased parent or sibling. If you need therapy, fine. Therapy helps. But it never hurts to use a little magic to ease your pain, as well.

♥ Spell to Ease a Family Quarrel

No matter how loving a family is, any time you have more than one person living in a single household, there will be quarrels. This spell can return harmony to the family by helping those involved to calm down. You'll need:

3 light blue candles (blue is the color of calm emotions
    and healing)
3 pieces of unlined blue paper
Peace oil (or olive oil)
Peace incense (or sandalwood)

This spell should be done on a Friday night. Inscribe each
candle with two of the following runes while visualizing the person who is the focus of the spell as being happy, calm, and relaxed. See any problems between the two of you resolved in a
way that promotes growth and understanding:

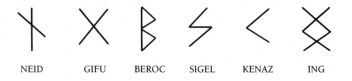

NEID   GIFU   BEROC   SIGEL   KENAZ   ING

Neid: to help calm distressed emotions
Gifu: to restore one's mental equilibrium and perspective
Beroc: to bring harmony back into the household
Sigel: to bring healing energy to all affected
Kenaz: to renew peace within the family
Ing: to bring a positive ending to the situation

Anoint each candle with the peace oil. As you do so, visualize you and the other person living happily and peacefully, and
chant three times for each candle:

> *Guardians of hearth, Guardians of home*
> *Stable as earth, stable as stone,*
> *Lend me your strength, lend me your calm*
> *Help me to make this magical balm*

Light the peace incense and light the candles. Write the person's name on each piece of paper with blue ink, and pass each
one in turn through the smoke of the incense and say:

As smoke fades to nothing, so does the anger that lies between [name] *and me. Let no harsh word or ill feeling remain that may cloud our minds or hearts.*

Light each piece of paper from a different candle and place in a fireproof receptacle. As you light each one chant three times:

> *Peace I send from me to you*
> *Love I send to follow through*
> *From this anger we are set free*
> *As I will, so shall it be!*

Let the candles burn out if possible. If it's not possible to let the candles burn themselves out, perform the spell on three consecutive nights, ending on Friday, and let the candles burn for two hours each night.

 Peace Oil

1 dram of olive oil as a base
10 drops lavender oil
10 drops rose oil
1 small piece of sodalite stone

Mix all ingredients any time during the waxing moon, with a Friday closest to the full moon being optimum. Empower by chanting nine times:

> *Gentle fragrance of fruit and flower*
> *I call upon your subtle power*
> *Bring to all a sense of peace*
> *So that strife may quickly cease.*

 Peace Incense

Powdered sandalwood
Pink rose petals

Lavender flowers
20 drops Peace Oil

Use the same procedure and chant as for Peace Oil, above.

To Renew Contact With Distant Loved Ones

In today's hectic world we all have dear friends or family members whom we haven't seen in quite a while. It seems that we just spoke with them, then suddenly we realize that "just spoke" was actually *ten years ago*. How long has it really been since you last called your best friend from high school? How about the last time your wrote that guy who helped you keep your sanity all through boot camp?

We've all had special people in our lives with whom, for whatever reason, we have lost contact. Even with computers and the miracle of e-mail, the demands of day-to-day life can make keeping in touch difficult. This spell can help reestablish the lines of communication. It should be done on a Wednesday (sacred day of Mercury, Roman God of Communication.) You'll need:

Blue candle
A pen with blue ink, pink paper, and a stamped envelope
   (the stamp signifies intent)
Friendship oil
Packing tape (wide cellophane type)

Carve the following runes down one side of the blue candle (blue is the color of communication), and your friend's name down the other:

ANSUZ   EIHWAZ   EOLH   WUNJO

Ansuz: to promote communication

Eihwaz: to remove any obstacles to that communication

Eolh: for friendship; it represents the "target" of one's communication

Wunjo: a "travel" rune, used to speed the energy of the spell safely on its way

As you carve the candle imagine yourself on the phone, chatting with your friend and catching up on all the things that have happened over the years. When you are done, anoint the candle with the friendship oil and chant at least seven times:

> *Friendship mine, friendship true,*
> *Friendship sent from me to you.*
> *Friendship strong, friendship free,*
> *Friendship sent from you to me.*

Now, use the pen and paper to write a letter to your friend. Tell the friend how happy you are to have reconnected with him or her, and how much you have missed his or her presence in your life. (Feel free to get as mushy and sentimental as you want; nobody is actually going to read this letter.) When finished, dab a little of the friendship oil onto both the letter and the envelope. Seal the envelope with wax from the blue candle. Be careful not to spill the hot wax on yourself.

Set the candle on top of the envelope (if the candle holder is stable enough for this, otherwise set the letter in front of the candle) and repeat the above chant seven more times. Let the candle burn out if possible, but let it burn for at least three hours.

Take the letter, the tape, and the friendship oil to your mailbox. Tape the letter securely to the inside of the mailbox; up against the top is best so that the mailman doesn't take it by accident. Anoint the opening of the mailbox with the friendship oil and repeat the friendship chant for a final seven times, then close the box. The mailbox will act to contain the spell's energy, letting it build up. Then each time the mailbox is opened, a concentrated "package" of magical energy will be released to do its work. As soon as contact is reestablished with your friend, remove the letter from the mailbox and put it someplace safe.

It should be noted that as you are trying to influence the life pattern of another person by reestablishing communication, free will and individual destiny comes into play. This spell will only work if renewed contact is in the best interest of all involved at the present time and under the current circumstances.

♥ Friendship Oil

1 dram of almond oil as a base
10 drops geranium oil
10 drops vanilla
10 drops ylang ylang
1 pinch grated lemon peel
2 whole cloves
1 small piece of turquoise

Mix all ingredients together any time during the waxing moon and empower by chanting seven times:

> *Friendships new and friendships old*
> *Friendships true and friendships bold*
> *More precious now than gold or gem*
> *May friendships never see an end!*

♥ Puppy Love

You can call on the assistance of your dragon allies to help you to find the perfect animal companion as well as the perfect human companion.

Small heart-shaped I.D. tag
1 pink candle

Generous supply of treats appropriate for the pet you are
looking for
Vanilla oil, or pure vanilla extract (for friendship)
Your dragon figurine

Inscribe the candle with a brief description of the type of pet
you are looking for: breed or species, age, and gender. Anoint
the candle with vanilla oil and chant three times:

> *Truly sees your dragon eyes*
> *All that dwells beneath the skies*
> *Help me separate from the rest*
> *The special pet that suits me best.*

Place the candle back in its holder and light it. Surround the
candle with the treats in the shape of a heart while repeating the
chant again three times. Now pick up the tag and paint the following rune, Eolh (for friendship), on one side:

Anoint the tag with the vanilla oil and again say the above
chant three times, bringing the total number of repeats to nine.
Place the tag next to the candle inside the heart and leave until
the candle burns out. When this is done, scoop up the treats
and put them in a separate bag. These will be the first treats you
give your new pet when you bring him/her home.

When you go looking for your new friend, take the tag with
you and hold it in your receptive hand (opposite from the one
you write with). As soon as you encounter the perfect pet the
tag will grow warm, or perhaps tingle, in your hand. *Note:* As
soon as possible after getting your new friend, have the tag engraved with your name, address, and phone number and attach
to your pet's collar if appropriate to the animal's species.

♥ *Time Capsule Spell*

We all have friends that we haven't seen in a while, and who may live distant from us, but that we love even though we don't see them that often. Teri, the owner of Salem's Artemesia Botanicals herb shop, recently got a call from an old friend and did the following spell. She had this to say:

At Yule a friend sent me a note that she hadn't heard from me in two years, and that a friendship of twenty-five years shouldn't end because of indifference. She was absolutely right. I was lazy. I had stuff going on, but so does everyone. So after meditating on it, I did this spell.

Get one of those pillows with one of those "friendship" sayings on it, or make your own. Take out some of the stuffing. In place of the stuffing, insert some mementos of the time you and your friend were together, things that have special meaning to the two of you. Here are the things that went into Teri's Time Capsule Pillow for Susan:

Arm band from the march on Washington
Potholder from their first apartment as roommates
Picture of the two of them from college
Piece of a blankie when they were pregnant together
Link from an old necklace Susan gave Teri
Recipe for escarole soup
Tie-dye bra (don't ask!)

One afternoon, Susan received a pillow that said FRIENDS ARE SPECIAL PEOPLE. Attached was a note that told her she would always be Teri's friend even and especially when they weren't near. Every time Susan looked at this pillow she would know Teri was thinking of her, because like that pillow, they were stuffed with memories.

Wish Beads

I'm a great fan of beads as magical tools.

Even as far back as the Stone Age—and I'm not saying that I remember that far back—beads were used as amulets or talismans against evil or to attract magical powers. Traditional Voodoo practitioners today wear beads in particular colors and patterns according to the *loa,* or spirits, that they honor. Native Americans wove beads into intricate patterns rich with spiritual symbolism. No self-respecting Egyptian would be caught dead in his tomb without masses of strands of beads to protect him as he made the dangerous journey to the Land of the Dead.

Beads can be made from gemstones, crystals, shells, rocks, clay, plastic, and glass. Necklaces of amber beads interspersed with glossy black jet beads are often worn by Wiccan priestesses, as both these substances generate electricity and traditionally carry magic power. The amber and jet necklace is the priestess's "badge of office" in some covens.

It's glass beads we'll be using in this simple, but very effective, spell which uses a string of colored glass beads to protect and bring good things to your friends and family. Fans of stained glass know that the effect of light shining through transparent colored glass is almost hypnotic, bringing a magic power of its own into a room.

The charm will be a string of beads with a protective crystal dangling from the end. Every few beads will be a good wish for your friend who receives the finished string, so plan your colors accordingly. You might use the magical color chart in chapter 1 as a guide, or use colors that seem right to you. If you want the Wish Bead string to have a particular purpose, such as healing, or happiness in an upcoming marriage, or good luck to a new baby, use colors appropriate to that purpose for your Wish Beads. You'll need:

- Glass beads in various sizes, shapes, and colors, but with large enough holes to take two or three thicknesses of thread. You can also combine the beads with small, drilled chips of gemstones, like quartz or agate.

- Nylon fishing line, or beading thread and a beading needle. The nylon line is easiest to use, although it hangs a little stiffly, but you won't have the bother of threading a needle: the beads slide right on.
- A clear crystal pendant drilled for hanging. Pure lead crystal cut into prisms is wonderful because when the light hits it, it throws rainbows around the room.
- 8-inch length of ribbon to use as a hanger for the finished bead string

Make your ribbon into a hanger for the Wish Bead string by simply tying it in a loop and making a neat bow at the top.

Decide how long you want to make the string of beads and add about eight inches to that. Tie the crystal onto the fishing line (I'm assuming you're using fishing line; if not, then run the beading needle through the hole in the crystal) and leave about three inches loose. As you string the first few inches of beads, you'll run the loose end back through them to hide it.

Start stringing your beads. Every third, seventh, or ninth bead (or whatever number you choose—3, 7, and 9 are magical numbers), make a good wish for the friend or family member to whom you'll be giving this string. These can be different wishes or the same wish repeated. You might make the beads you wish on larger than the others, or of a certain shape, or of a particular magical color or material, like an amber or quartz or garnet bead or chip, or a golden bead for luck or a purple one for peace. When you get to the end, tie the loose end tightly to the loop of colored ribbon near the bow, then run the loose end back through the beads to hide it. Hang the Wish Beads from the ribbon loop.

Then take the finished Wish Bead string in your hands and say this incantation:

By the power of the Goddess and God, I empower these beads to bring good luck, happiness, and [if you had a particular purpose in mind, name it here] *to* [name of person]. *This spell is done with harm to none.*

♥ *Witch's Cord for Family Protection*

We always want to keep bad things from our families and friends, even though we know that it's impossible to shelter them from everything. Hard times are unavoidable: The only good side in them is that they teach us lessons and strengthen us. However you want to cushion any blow as much as possible, and ward off any real evil or lasting problems.

See the general instructions for making Witch's Cords in chapter 1, then assemble the following:

  White cord, charged for protection and banishing fear
  Silver cord, charged for magic and the protection of the
    moon goddess
  Gold cord, charged for happiness and the protection of the
    sun god
  A small dram bottle filled with water. Water is the element of
    love and friendship and is a protective element
  A sprig of mistletoe, if you can find it. Mistletoe is a very
    protective herb. If it's the wrong season for mistletoe, use a
    small bag filled with rosemary or a cinnamon stick. Tie the
    herbs into the cord, and charge them for protection.

As you braid the cord, say this invocation:

By the powers of the Moon and Sun, by the power of the elements, I empower this cord to protect me and my family against trouble, fear, hardship, serious illness, and all forms of evil. If any trouble finds us, it's ill effects will be fleeting, and will only serve to draw us closer and add to our strength as a family. This spell is done with harm to none.

Hang the cord near the front or back doorway in the family home.

5

Becoming More Lovable

I'd never join any club that would have me as a member.
—Groucho Marx

If you've been turned down more often than a bedspread at a cheap motel, then you definitely need to start facing a harsh reality: It could be *you*.

And don't pass off that excuse that you just pick the wrong kind of person: It's still your decision to go with people you *know* are not good for you. If your problem is that no one is quite worthy of you, then the problem is still yours. If you're the best person you know, then you've been choosing your friends pretty poorly. Or else—you're afraid of the challenge.

If you have the deeply buried feeling that you're just not good enough, a feeling that pops to the surface only vaguely but still shows its ugly head from time to time, you have to start facing up to the reality that very few of us feel we're "good enough" across the board. Even the most confident people have those little soft voices that whisper to them on sleepless nights.

A friend of mine calls this the "Parade of Shame"—when you can't sleep and everything bad or dumb you ever did comes back to haunt you.

There's no reason you should let this insecurity get the better of you. Think of it as weeding the garden. You can't stop weeds from sneaking their way in, but you can root out those suckers before they take hold.

Self-Confident People

It's an old saying, but it's true that before you can get someone else to love you, you have to love yourself. Low self-esteem is like a bad perfume, and you can smell it coming a mile off.

People with confidence in themselves are more attractive. Looks are secondary when you've got it, and if you don't have it, looks won't make up for it. You could be the most beautiful person in the world, but if you're constantly putting yourself down, or you're a clingy, whiny, or demanding lover, that initial attraction fades fast.

Example: the Glenn Close character in *Fatal Attraction*. Ms. Close is a lovely woman and it was no wonder that her character had no trouble picking up a one-night stand, maybe even two nights. But even before the character went completely nuts, it was obvious that this was a woman who was going to be a liability sooner or later. And you don't even have to go to the movies to find people like this. Almost everyone knows a person who's physically attractive but just can't seem to hold on to love.

Now consider Lillian Hellman, one of the outstanding playwrights of the thirties and forties. Hellman wasn't exactly what you'd call physically attractive. In fact, she was kind of a woofer. But she had a string of lovers, most of whom were around for a long time, and who remained friends with her. Some stayed in love with her all their lives. What Hellman had, according to them, was a fascinating personality and extreme confidence in herself.

Mick Jagger isn't every young girl's dream in looks, but oh, baby! Does he make up for it in confidence and charisma!

Confidence and self-esteem is what separates life's winners from the losers, in love as with everything else.

Before you start doing spells to attract love, you should do spellwork to help you love yourself. And if you think this sounds self-indulgent and conceited, you're right. In fact, let's get rid of that word *conceited* anyway. It's a kid's word, a junior high school word, and it's caused a lot of trouble. Because of it, people are taught that to think highly of themselves is socially undesirable. You always see these little high school twits talking jealously about how someone is "conceited" when they know they'd kill to be with that person. And, in fact, if the "conceited" person pays any attention to them at all, they'll dump their friends for him or her faster than a week-old prom corsage.

Grown-up life is not all that different. We just call it "sucking up." And *conceited* is now *self-assured*. And self-assured people also know when a little humility makes them look even better. It's part of their charm.

Don't misunderstand and confuse *self-assured* with *pompous.* Pompous people are pains in the ass. They're constantly bragging and can't stop talking about themselves and how wonderful everyone thinks they are. Pompous people have to keep the conversation about themselves, hoping that someone will believe it. They need—they *must have*—followers, sycophants who will agree with their every word and tell them how wonderful they are. You see a lot of pompous asses with mousy wives or husbands who don't dare disagree with them. What fun is a mate like that?

Self-assured people don't have to say a word. Rich or poor, famous or private, their confidence shines through. They can admit mistakes, can apologize, can back off from a position they find is no longer valid, and they can do it with style and without losing an ounce of self-assurance. That's because they believe that everything they do is right *for them*, and if it isn't right, they'll make it right even if it means starting over. They're gracious losers as well as gracious winners.

Self-assured people are not threatened by other people or by adverse opinions or disagreements. They do not need universal approval because they have their own approval of themselves, and it's unshakable. They do not need fame or notoriety. They do not become obsessed with "getting even." They listen to opinions, but feel that they can reject or accept them as they see fit. They are secretly convinced that they're superior to many people, but they'd never, never show it. They're gracious and charming, but if they have to deal with idiots they do it quickly and efficiently, and then never think of that person again, since idiots do not figure in their lives. And the idiots are usually totally unaware that they've been dismissed as insignificant. Self-assured people have lovely manners.

Truly self-assured people are very open to others. They assume the best about people and are happy when that assumption is proved right. They have something to give, and are not just looking to take, but they love to learn from other people. That openness, and their attitude of equality with their peers is what attracts people to them: They make other people feel valued.

They're just great, and I advise you to become one of them as quickly as possible, through magical means or otherwise. Start with spells for loving yourself.

♥ *Quick Overnight Spell for Self-Confidence*

For this spell you will need a purple eyeliner pencil. Before you go to bed, use the eyeliner pencil to draw the following runes either over your solar plexus chakra (right above your belly button), or over your "third eye" chakra (centered slightly above your eyebrows):

X

GIFU   SIGEL   MANNAZ

Gifu: to help restore the balance between one's mind and
   body

Sigel: to help build one's self-confidence and increase one's
   stamina

Mannaz: to focus one's thoughts and to sharpen one's mind

Stand in front of a mirror and look yourself in the eye and
say out loud:

*I am strong, confident, and capable. When I wake in the morning
I will take charge of my life with joy and I will perform one action
For no other purpose than to make myself happy.*

When you wake in the morning, wash off the eyeliner, confident
that the power of the runes has worked their magic for you. Be
sure to perform your one action with no thought as to whether
or not it is "bad" for you (Make sure to use common sense here.
There's a *big* difference between eating a thick piece of double
chocolate cake or spending two hours in a bubble bath instead
of the gym, and doing something illegal or dangerous.)

Perform this spell whenever you feel the need for a little boost,
before an important meeting, presentation, exam, or interview.

Dragon Spell for Self-Confidence:

Another powerful Dragon Spell from the Clan of the Dragon.
For this one, you'll need:

Iron shavings (strength)

One each of citrine (self-determination), rose quartz (self-
   esteem), and amethyst (courage)

Cinnamon (personal power), bay (success), catnip
   (happiness)

Candles: 1 red, 1 purple, 1 orange

4-inch × 4-inch black cloth square (black repels negativity)

Red, orange, and purple thread

Gold fabric paint and brush, or gold paint pen (gold for
   power)
Dragons blood oil
Scribing tool (an awl, heavy needle, straight pin, etc.)
Your dragon figurine

First place the dragon figurine where it can overlook your
workspace. Dragons are *extremely* nosy and like to know what's
going on at all times. Inscribe the candles with the following
words: *strength* on the red candle; *self-assurance* on the purple;
success on the orange. Anoint each candle with the dragons
blood oil and chant three times:

> *Dragons of Power, Dragons of Light*
> *Dragons of Wisdom, Dragons of Night*
> *Lend me your magic, lend me your aid*
> *Lend me your guidance as this spell is made!*

Place the candles in their holders and light. Using the gold fabric paint or gold paint pen, draw the following runes on one side
of the black cloth and let dry. This will be the outside of the bag.

SIGEL   LAGAZ   ISA

Sigel: for strength and self-confidence
Lagaz: for increased vitality and life-force
Isa: for development of will

Charge the first four items according to the indicated qualities
and place them in the center of the cloth. Gather the four corners together and tie shut using the red, orange, and purple
thread. Pass the bag carefully over each candle and say:

[Red] *for courage* [Orange] *for success* [Purple] *for self assurance*

Finally, visualize a stream of electric blue energy coming from your dragon figurine and enveloping you and your bag. Feel yourself filling with the strength and confidence of a dragon. Repeat the dragon chant three times or until you "see" the bag pulsate with energy. Meditate on your new sense of confidence for a few minutes then hang the bag where it will be the first thing you see in the morning and the last thing you see at night. Remember to thank the dragon spirits for their assistance.

Loving Yourself

With every great blessing comes a responsibility. This is the lesson of Epona, Celtic Goddess of Horses. This goddess was so powerful that the conquering Romans adopted her into their own pantheon, with an official feast day of December 18. This lovely oil is by Jane Raeburn, the ritual by Cassius Julianus of the Julian Society.

♥ *Epona's Oil*

Base: Grapeseed oil, use as much or as little as you need to
  get the desired strength
7 drops balsam peru oil
7 drops fir-needle oil
14 drops nutmeg oil
3 drops vanilla oil
3 drops pine oil
1 pinch lavender buds
1 pinch balsam needles

In the ancient world, a horse represented freedom, power, and wealth, but also required much drudgery and daily care.

Consider a blessing for which you are working, and consider also the responsibility that goes with it. If you seek love, are you willing to take on the responsibility of giving and communicating? If you seek wealth, are you willing to take on the responsibility of stewardship and wise investing? If you seek health, are you willing to change your habits to take better care of your body?

Now, anoint a green candle with this Epona oil. Also prepare a cookie or small cake and a glass of wine or juice.

Go to your altar, or a place sacred to you. Place the candle in the center of the altar, the chalice to the left, and the cake to the right. Focus within for a moment to prepare yourself.

Light the candle and say:

I light this flame in honor of the goddess Epona. May her love, fruitfulness, and protection be manifested in this place.

Now call on Epona by saying:

Epona, Goddess of Horses, I invite thee to be here with me. Noble Lady, I call upon you; share with me your protection, your abundance, and your powers of freedom. I welcome thee! Hail Epona!

Speak your need to Epona in your own words. You may wish to ask for her help in reaching a goal, for some needed thing or situation, or simply for inspiration and guidance. Remember to accept responsibility to use her gifts wisely.

When you have finished, take up the chalice and say:

May the blessings of Epona be with me.

Drink from the chalice. Then hold up the small cake and say:

May the abundance of Epona be with me.

Take a small bite of the cake. End the rite by saying:

Epona, I give thanks to thee for thy blessings and for thy presence. Hail and Farewell, noble goddess!

Allow the candle to burn out.

Later, place the cake in an outdoor place, and pour the wine onto the ground beside it. Say:

Epona, accept this offering of love and trust. Hail to thee!

Meghan's Cord for Self-Confidence

This is another pretty and very useful spell from Teri at Artemisia Botanicals. Teri said, "My daughter, Meghan, was having trouble in school and decided that she wanted to make a Witch's Cord to help her do better. When working with kids, it's good to get them to express their feelings about what they want. Meg thought that she wasn't as smart as everyone else. She also figured that if she was psychic, she wouldn't have to study or do schoolwork (that was a big discussion!). What we came up with was a cord just for her, and it still hangs in our living room."

Meghan's Cord is a wonderful cord for anyone needing more self-confidence, no matter how old you are. It's a daily reminder that you're as great as you want to be. You'll notice that on this cord are objects especially for Meghan—objects that reinforced her confidence and told her that she was a winner. You'll want to substitute objects that have that meaning for you. Here's what Meghan used on her cord:

9 feet of pink cord, for self-love
9 feet of white cord, to banish thoughts of inferiority
Tarot cards:
> The Empress (because it's good to be the Queen. Use
> the Emperor if you're a guy)
> The 8 of wands (or a card or cards equivalent to your age)
A pentacle she had won at a fair
A pencil for help in school

A test paper on which she had gotten an A

♥ Witch's Cord for the Child Within

Many years ago, Teri worked in a magical shop here in Salem. One day a woman came in and Teri said she felt such overwhelming sadness from this woman, a sense of a frightened child. Later, she found out that the woman had been an abused child: She had grown up, but that small scared child was still with her. Teri did this spell to protect and love a child, or for the child inside, letting the child know it is worthy of love.

9 feet of black cord, to draw in good energy
9 feet of white cord, to banish negativity or fear
9 feet of pink cord, for self-love (also may add light blue for boys)

Braid the cords together, then add a small dragon at the top to be a friend and protector. Hang childhood objects on the cord: small toys from fast food restaurants, dinosaurs, blocks with messages, crayons, any object that delights a child and makes the cord fun.

Charge the entire cord for banishing the fear that stands in the way of self-love.

♥ Solar Confidence Oil

15 drops cedar oil
10 drops cinnamon oil
10 drops saffron oil
1 pinch marigold petals
1 pinch grated orange peel
1 small citrine

Mix all ingredients together on a Sunday at solar zenith (not necessarily 12 noon; check your almanac) and chant seven times:

Bright Star of Life, O Heavenly Fire,
Hearken to me, hear my desire!
As brilliant as you, pray let me be
Confidence mine, the whole world to see!

♥ Simple Talisman for Self-Esteem

In 1915, Emile Coué, in his *On Suggestion and Its Applications,* told his patients to repeat this phrase fifteen to twenty times, in the morning and in the evening: "Every day in every way, I'm getting better and better."

Today, we'd call it a positive affirmation. Who cares what you call it as long as it works for you and you believe it? Say it often enough, and it might well come true. The power of suggestion is very real. If you believe you're a loser, then don't be surprised if you keep sabotaging yourself. If you begin to believe you're a winner, don't be surprised if good things are attracted to your new energy.

It helps to have a focus for good thoughts about yourself, something to trigger your sense of self-confidence.

Certain stones are thought to promote self-confidence, just by wearing or carrying them. One of the best is a sapphire, which is said to bring its owner health, strength, intelligence, and social success. However, it also promotes chastity, so you know . . . your social success in certain areas may be limited. And sapphires are expensive.

Instead, try carrying an agate. Agates have varying properties according to their colors, but the Persians believed that all agates promote eloquence, bring good fortune and wealth from legacies, and enhance the good side of your personality. Tawny agate brings luck in love and increases intelligence.

Garnets are also believed to increase self-confidence. Rose quartz is always good for self-love.

Whichever stone you choose to carry as a talisman, you should empower it by this method:

Light a yellow candle for success and confidence. While staring into the flame of the candle, hold your selected talisman between your hands and feel the power of success, self-confidence, self-control, and all the good things in you that you want to make stronger. See your power as a million tiny stars, all glittering with electric energy. As the power flows through you, through your body and bloodstream and brain and heart, you can feel it as a million sparks inside you, restoring you, energizing you, burning away the old insecurities and giving you a newer, stronger glow. Just bask in that feeling for a few minutes, letting some of the power into the talisman.

After a few minutes, blow out the candle and relax.

From now on, when you wear, carry, touch, or look at your talisman stone, you'll feel that surge of energy and self-confidence.

6

Great Balls o' Fire!
White Trash Love Spells

I get very upset when I hear people knock white trash.

It's not just the use of the implied perjorative that I dislike. No. It's the fact that American culture owes white trash a debt that we can never repay. Without white trash, we would be without some of our most treasured cultural institutions. Jerry Lee Lewis springs immediately to mind.

There'd be no big-eyed kid paintings on velvet. The iridescent blue eyeshadow industry would grind to a halt, and small-town beauty pageants would end. Televangelists would be preaching to dead air—in fact, they wouldn't exist at all. Big hair would be simply a wistful memory. The literary scandal of the 1950s, *Peyton Place,* would never have been written, since Grace Metalious wrote it about actual trashy people she knew in Gilmanton, New Hampshire. The films of John Waters would never have been made without the trashiest people in Baltimore. And we'd never again see the epitome of White Trash Fashion: short shorts worn with spike heels by a bleached blonde with a cigarette hanging out of one side of her mouth and dragging a whiny four-year-old by the arm across the A&P parking lot and pissed off because she's late for Free Beer Night at the bowling alley.

Although the mecca of white trash, the holy of holies, is Las Vegas, white trash knows no economic or regional boundaries. There's poor white trash and rich white trash. White trash is a part of life from the West Coast to the East, from Alabama to New York and a whole big chunk of Vermont and Maine. A friend of mine in Redding, California, says that the entire town is founded on a bedrock of white trash. And even though the traditional grammatical usage is "white trash," in actuality, blacks, Hispanics, Native Americans, and Asians have a god-given, constitutional right to be as trashy as white folks. As long as you're living in America and appreciate bad taste, you can be part of the melting pot.

If you're tempted to put down white trash contributions to the American scene, just remember this: Without white trash *there would be no Elvis!*

In fact, so strongly associated with white trash is Elvis, and such is his power for strong romantic emotion, that almost *all* white trash love spells include invoking the power of his name and his energy. This was a man who was faithful. He loved three women with a pure and burnin' love: his Momma, Priscilla, and his daughter. He was, is, and always will be the King, not only of rock 'n' roll, but of White Trash Romance.

So let's just get over this prejudice against white trash and acknowledge it for the many contributions that it's made to our post-TV nation.

Most of these spells, naturally, are from the Sisterhood of Thalia in Salem, who take their humorous spells very seriously. One important side note: The Sisters say that cheap perfume— the sleazier the better, but not so cheap that it makes you hurl— makes great spritzed incense for white trash spells.

One-Night Stands

Why would any self-respecting person want a spell for a one-night stand? They're so degrading, you say; they're dangerous, the people involved are just looking for a quick thrill.

And exactly what's wrong with a quick thrill? Cheap thrills are better than no thrills at all.

A one-night romance doesn't have to be grubby or degrading or dangerous, provided you use a little caution and think ahead. And when I talk about one-night stands, I don't mean with someone you just met in a bar and have known for a couple of hours, but through a haze of margaritas and rampant hormones he or she looks reeeeeal good. Damn, didn't you people see *Fatal Attraction*?

Instead, I'm talking about sex with someone you know, and the two of you decide to give it a go one night when the time is right, with no regrets or ties or embarrassment afterward. It's more like sex between friends. And, admittedly, not everyone can pull it off.

But for those who can, one-night stands can make beautiful memories.

Here's a good affirmation for a one-night stand.

By the power that is Elvis, tonight will be filled with romance, thrills both quick and otherwise, and good feelings between me and [name]. *When the night is over and the morning comes, there will be no jealousies, hard feelings, regrets, or nasty gossip. This spell is done with harm to none.*

Wear your good underwear and have a nice time!

Boinkin' in the Back Seat and Pumpin' in the Pickup

If you've ever savored the nasty little thrill of doing it in the backseat, you can thank white trash culture. When you're an adult, nothing's as low-rent as the backseat, unless it's the bed of the pickup. Snaggin' your shorts on the gun rack is the ultimate in the white trash experience.

Want to live dangerously? Want your romance with a giddy *frisson* of exhibitionism, and the possibility of arrest? Want to feel like you're sixteen again?

If you've got a car, then you're set for an evening of white trash love in the finest American tradition. Even better if you have a pickup truck, but be a gentleman—vacuum up the hound dog hairs first and remove the beer cans: Ladies appreciate that little touch of class. And make sure nobody else's underwear is in the glove compartment when you're rummaging through it for the condoms.

For true backseat love, we have the following spell in the form of a Witch's Cord.

Witch's Cord for Vehicular Romance

Now, for this, you're going to have to remove the fuzzy dice from the rearview mirror, or at least make room for the cord.

The basic Witch's Cord may be made of ribbons, cord, or yarn to match the vehicle's interior, plus the red for passion and white for protection. Hell, this is white trash we're talking about—you can even make it out of that plastic gimp lacing that the kids use. Make it a lot shorter than the usual cord, so it doesn't tangle in the stick shift or catch fire from the ashtray. Tie the following onto the cord:

- Cardboard air freshener, preferably in a jasmine, lavender, or rose scent, for female energy
- Cardboard air freshener in pine scent, for male energy
- 1 piece of hematite, onyx, obsidian, or any black stone, for invisibility from the police cruiser
- If you're married and you have the bride's garter from your wedding, this is a prime place to hang it. (But you better be in the car with who you're married to, you scamp!)

Empower the cord with magic by invoking the following spell:

By the power that is Elvis, I charge this cord to protect me and my [man/woman] as we consummate our true love in the back seat of this, our solemn and sacred vehicle. Give us passion and power, protect us from police scrutiny or nosy neighbors, and protect us from pulled muscles. This spell is done with harm to none.

♥   *"Cheatin' Heart" Spell to Get Over an Unfaithful Lover*

You'll like this spell. It involves eatin' and cheatin', two time-honored activities. And if you've never heard Kinky Friedman and the Texas Jewboys' song about that, "Waitress, Oh Waitress," I'm sure not gonna quote it here. They got laws about that kind of stuff.

First, you've got to find the recording of Hank Williams's "Your Cheatin' Heart." I don't care if it takes you a month, you really, really need it. In the first place, the lyrics say it all about lyin' lovers who are gonna get what's coming to them. You'll be very gratified to hear it, I guarantee. The entire song is about "what goes around comes around," which always makes us feel better.

Okay, so you're listening to the record and you're thinking about that lyin', cheatin' redneck sumbitch and maybe you're crying and upset and all. That's fine. You probably still need to do that.

But here's what else you do. Get you two gingerbread people, one boy and one girl. One of these is you. The other is someone you haven't met. Since living well is the best revenge, let the two gingerbread people dance to the music of the record. Picture you and a new love dancing, doing the Texas Two-Step, having a couple of tequila shots, sharing the worm at the bottom of the bottle, going to the movies, whatever you like to do. See yourself happy and having fun.

Say this spell:

By the power that is Elvis (and Hank Williams), I banish all the
hurt, anger, and bad feelings associated with that cheatin' loser.
I make this spell to draw a new, happy, faithful lover into my life.

When the record is over, you can eat the gingerbread people.
This is the best part.

How to Get Married
(to someone other than your cousin)

We're into the realm of folk magic here. You know when an-
thropologists go poking around in the Ozarks or the backwoods
of Vermont or somewhere and find this entire town that nobody
knew existed and everybody who lives there are cousins and
they all talk about "the olden ways"? That kind of folk magic.

One of the oldest spells involves an apple and a mirror. At
midnight on Halloween night, by the light of a single candle, eat
the apple in front of the mirror. When the apple's gone, you'll
see the face of the person you're going to marry.

Another also involves an apple. (Apples are very big in folk
magic dealing with love. I think it goes back to apples being sacred to Venus and Diana—who knows *where* those backwoods-
type people came from originally?) You core the apple, write your
wish to get married on a small piece of paper, then stash the apple
under your bed for three nights. And hope you don't have mice.

If you want to get married, borrow a friend's wedding ring.
Light three white candles and pass the ring very quickly through
the flame of all three. Better not tell your friend that you're
sticking her five-thousand-dollar diamond solitaire in the fire.

Here's a voodoo marriage spell. Take the juice of four lemons
and rub the legs of the bed with the juice for nine nights. Put
a glass of water under the bed. When you get in bed, lie with
your knees bent and your legs spread. (We'll just assume you're
sleeping alone. If you're not, you might be rudely interrupted in

this position.) Keep repeating your wish to get married until you fall asleep.

♥ Jethro's "I Like 'Em Big and Dumb" Spell

Jethro Bodine was the built-like-a-brick-outhouse nephew on *The Beverly Hillbillies*. Jethro wasn't what you'd call heavy in the I.Q. department, but he had a body that made strong women swoon and gay men faint. You could definitely see yourself ripping the clothes off this boy and playing Wild West Rodeo Rider. Who cares if you'd have to throw a paper bag over his brain?

If you've just broken up with your last boyfriend, who scored sixteen million on his SATs and discovered a new element in the periodic table, but who treated you like you were something he grew in a petri dish, you might just be looking for someone a little less intellectually refined. Someone earthy. Someone who'd just shut up and hump all night until the sheets catch fire from friction. Is that too much to ask? I thought not.

Remember, you're not looking for Ahnold here—he's too smart. What you want is more along the lines of Steve Reeves, who was in all those Italian-made Hercules movies in the sixties. He wore this tiny loincloth and his voice was always dubbed in—who knew if he could even talk? Who cared?

For this Fire Spell (read the basics in chapter 1) you'll need:

A magazine picture of the hunkiest male you can find. If you're a Fabio fan, you've got it licked: Just rip the cover off your favorite romance novel.
Amber oil, charged to bring a lover
Red candle, charged to bring a lover
Red ink, charged for bringing a lover, and plain paper
Any of the Love Incenses from this book, but the Sisterhood of Thalia's Lust Incense in chapter 2 comes highly recommended

Light the candle. Get the charcoal going and add some of the incense. Say:

Hercules and Apollo, I offer you this incense as thanks for your aid in doing this spell to bring me my desire.

With the red ink, write on the picture of the stud muffin: "I want one a' *these!*" It helps to be direct. Touch the amber oil to the four corners of the picture, and over the heart and genitals (remember our goals, now!) of the photo.

Write this spell on the paper:

By the power of Hercules and Apollo, I make this spell to bring me a lover who is big, strong, with a great body, not too smart, kind, heterosexual [or gay, your choice], with gentle temperament, and a good lover. This spell is done with harm to none.

Burn the picture, and as it burns read the spell aloud. Then burn the spell and toss a little incense into the fire. While everything burns, visualize yourself bouncing on the Beautyrest with a guy like this.

Depending on your tolerance level, you might want to combine this with the One-Night Stands spell. Or not.

Mending Feelings After a Breakup: The Lesser Banishing Ritual of Elvis

Okay, so maybe you didn't have a successful marriage. That doesn't mean you can't have a successful divorce.

Breaking up is hard, and there's always resentment involved. But if you let that resentment tear you up, you both lose. Oh sure, after a breakup you tell your close friends that your former beloved was a true bitch/bastard, the loser *di tutti* losers, lower than a snake in a wagon rut, and they agree sympathetically because they're your friends. But after a while, even your closest friend will definitely wish you'd just get over it and get on with it.

Keeping the anger boiling isn't going to help your kids, either.

But this is the most convincing argument I can think of for getting over a breakup: *Elvis and Priscilla managed to get a dee-vorce and still speak to each other like civilized folks,* and so can you. Do you actually have the presumption to believe yourself better than Lord Elvis and Lady Priscilla?

Read this entire spell closely and think about it before you do it. That's the only way to know exactly what you're going to need. It's designed to banish those feelings that are still making you miserable and strengthen the cooperation between you.

For this spell, you're going to need some paper and a pen. And this is a fire spell, so be prepared to burn the paper, and it could be a *lot* of paper, depending on how pissed off you are. And do this spell while you're alone, because there could be some yelling and hollering involved.

Write down on the paper everything you hate about the person you broke up with, everything he or she did to you, and everything that angered you. So it takes more than one piece of paper—who cares? Just get it all out.

When you've got it all written down, hold the paper in your hands and think about what you've written, read it out loud if you want to, and just let your anger pour out of you and into the paper. If it helps to yell and curse and cry, don't be shy—let 'er rip. You're alone, right? If you don't want the neighbors to call the cops, put a pillow over your face and yell right into it.

When you've got it all out, repeat this spell:

Into this paper, I pour my anger, my pain, my loss, my sense of betrayal and all the other harmful emotions connected with our breakup. It leaves me, and goes into this paper.

Really feel it go in there, too. Feel everything drain out of you, and feel yourself relax.

Now burn the paper. And as you burn it, feel all that resentment burning up with it as you burn the past and get ready to build a new life on the ashes. While you watch it burn, say:

This is an end to my anger, my pain, my loss, my sense of betrayal and all the other harmful emotions connected with our breakup.

When the fire cools, take the ashes outside and let the wind carry them off.

Now here's the healing part. You'll do this right away, or you can give it a couple of days. Go through the house and pick up a few little things that meant something to you and your lover, things you used in the happy times. If you don't have anything, then make another list and write it down. Take your list, or whatever object you've found, and put it in a light blue bag or wrap it in a square of light blue fabric. Light blue, because that's the color that numbs pain so you can heal. As you put it in the bag, let yourself think back on the good times, on what brought you two together in the first place. And while you do this, let yourself realize that no matter how bad things got, there was some good too, and that you were both only human.

Put this bag or bundle somewhere where you can see it for a while, and when the anger seems about to take you over again, look at it and let the memories help you get your balance back.

Oh, and it helps a lot if you can afford to treat yourself to a weekend in Las Vegas to get over it. If you can't do that, listen to some Elvis records. The happy ones, not "Are You Lonesome Tonight?" or anything like that. On vinyl.

7

Historical Love Spells: Don't Try These at Home!

By the pricking of my thumbs,
Something wicked this way comes.
—Second Witch, *Macbeth,* iv:i

Voodoo Love Spells

There are some interesting love spells from historical archives, but the most intriguing belong to the great New Orleans Voodoo queen, Marie Laveau, who practically ran the city in the eighty years of her reign.

I've included the Voodoo spells in this chapter (which also includes black magic spells) because of their historical connection with Marie Laveau. And because, frankly, they didn't fit anywhere else. But I do want to say that Voodoo is in no way to be considered black magic or "evil," no matter what you saw in those grade-B zombie movies. Voodoo is a complex religion, not easily understood by outsiders, and what we don't understand we tend to mistrust. But if you described the Roman Catholic rite of transubstantiation to someone who'd never heard of it, they'd probably be horrified to learn that Holy

Communion consists of drinking the blood and eating the body of a god.

Voodoo was brought to New Orleans by slaves from Africa, and slaves and free people of color fleeing the slave revolts of Saint Domingue (now Haiti) in 1791. Voodoo is much older than that, with roots deep in African culture. It was and still is a religion of the people, one in which the living and the spirits live in respect and harmony. The drums, dancing, and movements of Voodoo rites draw the believers into a closer relationship with the *loa,* their gods and spirits, giving them strength and confidence. It is a religion of joy, rather than repression.

Needless to say, Voodoo terrified the Christian church and threatened the slaveowner economy that Christianity reinforced, and the practice was outlawed. Voodoo believers were forced to convert and, being mainly slaves, they had little choice. However, *saying* you believe in a forced religion and *actually* believing in it are two different things. The Voodoos merely found Christian saints that embodied many of the traits of the Voodoo spirits, and told the slaveowners that they indeed worshipped the saints when they were in fact still worshipping the *loa* and merely using the saint's statue as a focus for the true power of Erzulie or Legba.

Marie Laveau included a great deal of practicality in her practice of Voodoo. She saw no reason why Voodoo and Catholicism couldn't coexist, and so wove the two tightly together. Catholic priests in New Orleans learned not to question their congregations too closely on what they did on Saturday night before Sunday mass. Many a good Catholic also considered him or herself a good Voodoo.

The great Voodoo queen was actually two women, mother and daughter: When the first Marie grew too old to preside, the second took over her duties. The first Marie was born about 1794 as a free woman of color. She was a hairdresser, and her biographers think that was the real key to Marie's extraordinary hold over the city. Millionaires, politicians, policemen, judges, and the ordinary people of the city were all respectful of Marie, because she seemed to know *everybody's* dirty little secrets

Then, even more than now, women talked to their hairdressers, and since the hairdressers of Marie's day came to the houses to practice their professions, Marie probably heard a great deal of backstairs gossip from the servants, too. Knowledge is power, and Marie had plenty. Both Maries knew the value of good PR: when the Voodoo rituals of St. John's Eve, the most important day of the Voodoo calendar, were celebrated at Bayou St. John, Marie invited the press, the public, and the police. It didn't hurt, either, that both mother and daughter had extraordinary charisma.

If you wanted magic for a lover, a husband, a death, a curse, or the removal of a curse, you went to Marie Laveau. There was simply no one else that mattered. Even today, believers go to St. Louis Cemetery No. 1 and leave offerings and chalked crosses on Marie Laveau's tomb, asking for her assistance. I remember being taken there as a child by my father, a Louisiana native and a believer, and told to make a wish.

Voodoo is a religion that never died out; it's still hale and hearty in many countries and in big American cities, including its American mecca, New Orleans. The kind of hybrid Voodoo practiced by Marie Laveau has largely given way to the restoration of the older, purer, more spiritually centered religion of Africa and Haiti, and is one of the most interesting religions being practiced today.

Marie Laveau had a brisk business in love potions, powders, and spells. Here are three of her most famous techniques.

♥ Marie Laveau's Spell for a Straying Lover

To keep a man or woman faithful, take a towel that the two of you have used when you made love. When the lover is asleep, wave the towel in his/her face and ask the spirits to keep the lover faithful to you.

♥ *Marie Laveau's Fidelity Spell for Women*

Okay, you women are going to have to *really* be at your wit's end for this one, because it's mucho disgusting. But here it is: If you want your man to be faithful for all time, secretly mix some of your menstrual blood into his food. This not only keeps him home, it keeps him totally whipped, if you get my meaning.

Marie Laveau doesn't add this, but I'd offer the guy a little Mylanta afterward. Actually, in the age of AIDS, this spell is pretty irresponsible. But it's still in effect in some quarters of New Orleans, and just the thought of it keeps most guys in line. Actually, if your cooking is so bad that the man wouldn't notice, you've got more problems than this spell will cure.

♥ *Marie Laveau's Love Spell*

A girl wanting a specific man to love her would bring one of the man's gloves to Marie. The Voodoo queen would fill it with sugar and honey to sweeten the man, and steel dust for magical power. The girl had to sleep with the glove under her mattress. And presumably a Roach Motel under the bed because of all that honey and sugar.

Black Magic

I thought long and hard about some of the following spells, because they involve what most Witches would call black magic. But I've found that even if you tell people not to do magic that manipulates the free will of others, they're going to do it anyway. However, you'll notice that I'm not giving the exact method of doing the spells. Except for the Slavic flowerpot spell, because it's just so Mary Poppins. Some of them we just don't know; some are too gross, some are way too complex and take a year or more of preparation.

The best I can do is stress the karmic implications. If you go this route, you'd better enjoy what you get because you're going to pay a price for what you want. And I don't mean eventually— like in the few seconds before you die or in the afterlife, although you could well end up still making those karmic payments after you're dead—but sooner than you think. And don't be thinking that you can make some kind of loophole to get out of it. You can't.

Usually, using magic to win the love of a specific person doesn't work. And the few times it does work, the path of true love doesn't run very smoothly. This is because it never is *true* love: someone who is forced to come to you isn't coming out of love or free will, he or she is coming as a result of psychic rape. But hey, if you have no problem with that and you're willing to settle for a sleazy substitute for the real thing, be my guest. Just remember the Threefold Law of Karma: What you do comes back to you three times.

♥ The Flowerpot Spell

This is a love spell from the Slavs. It qualifies as black magic, from the Witches' point of view, because it's manipulative magic, but it's still kinda cute.

If you've got the hots for a guy, find his footprint and dig up the dirt around it. Put it in a flowerpot and plant marigolds in it. The reason for marigolds is that they're thought to be a flower that never fades. (They *die,* of course, they just stay nice-looking until they do. In my opinion, these flowers are a total waste in a love spell—better to use them in a youth and beauty antiaging spell.) As the marigolds bloom and never fade, the guy's love also blooms and endures.

Those Slavic girls better make sure this guy is the One. Nothing's worse than getting bored with a lover who can't go away because he's bewitched into sticking around. This is another reason why manipulative magic sucks: You can't tell how it's going to turn out.

♥ Dr. John Fian's Love Spell

One of the most likable workers of love magic was Dr. John Fian, a Scotsman who lived around 1590. Dr. Fian was hopelessly in love with the sister of one of his students. He made a deal with the student to obtain three of the young woman's pubic hairs for him, so he could work his spell to gain her love. However, the boy wasn't very good at covert operations: He sneaked up on his sister when she was sleeping, but instead of cutting the hairs, he decided to pluck them, which woke his sister and the entire house.

The boy went to the fields and found a young heifer. This time he took a pair of shears—what a dolt—and clipped three hairs.

Fian was just thrilled and set right to work doing his spell, enchanting the hairs, muttering incantations, anticipating the happy nights to come.

The spell worked really well, too. Pretty soon, the heifer was following Fian everywhere. As the old text says, the heifer "made toward the schoolmaster, leaping and dancing upon him."

He became a laughingstock, but no one was laughing harder than Fian. He admitted what he'd done and the mistake he'd made, good-natured to the end.

And the end was to come very quickly. Fian was accused of witchcraft by that fanatic, King James I, who personally supervised Fian's torture. I think I mentioned that there was a price to be paid for black magic, but this seems all out of proportion to the offense. A leather thong was fastened around Fian's forehead and tightened until the blood flowed, then his head was jerked in all directions. His legs were slowly crushed in a vise and pins stuck through his tongue to make him confess. And he did confess.

Amazingly Fian escaped from prison and publicly recanted his confession, which infuriated King James. When he was re-captured, the king invented new tortures just for him. His fingernails were pulled out and pins stuck through the fingers, his legs put again in the vises and crushed with hammer blows until they were pulp—to make sure he'd never escape again—and he was subjected to five more weeks of torture, under the delighted eyes of good King James (yeah, the Bible guy) who was doing this for the Lord, then burned to death in Edinburgh on Castle Hill. He insisted to the end that his confession had been a forced lie.

Oddly enough, King James, who was paranoid on the subject of demonology, who saw devils and witches in every shadow and caused thousands of people to be tortured and murdered in Britain and later in the American colonies, grew bored with the subject and went on to other interests. The witch accusations and trials continued, however. They were just good business by then.

Faust's Deal With Mephistopheles
for Helen of Troy

Faust was a man who wanted everything. Youth, wealth, looks, power, and a hot babe.

Unfortunately, the hot babe he wanted not only belonged to someone else—she was dead. Had been dead, in fact, for a thousand years.

The story varies, and has been told by Goethe, Marlowe, and in an opera by Gounod, but historical evidence points to there having been a real Faustus, a kind of freelance thaumaturge. Whether he had dealings with the Devil is in doubt, but he did make it clear that he possessed dark and ancient secrets.

When Faustus sold his soul to Mephistopheles (the Devil, as he's known among the televangelist crowd), he was less interested in acquiring the *knowledge* of all things than he was in acquiring the *experience* of all things. One of the things he asked Mephistopheles to do was to restore his youth (he had been a dirty old man) so that he could seduce a young girl. He was successful; the girl had a child and was so distraught over her disgrace that she drowned the baby and went to prison to await hanging. She went completely mad there. This whole Love Spell did not work out the way Faust had thought it would, and the Prince of Darkness—as usual—got the best of the deal.

Faust, who for a smart guy really acted like a complete jerk, continued to work with Mephistopheles. This time, he wanted to see all the famous beauties of history and the one he was most interested in seeing was Helen of Troy. Once again, he promised Mephistopheles anything; even eternal damnation was not too high a price to pay. The Trojan War was fought for Helen, who was supposedly the most beautiful woman in the world. Mephistopheles conjured up the ghosts of the fabulous ladies. Not content to just *look* at Helen, Faust fell in love with her and actually tried to make love to her. Doing it with the dead is almost never a good idea, and Faust was transported directly to Hell (in the opera with much fabulous music and flames and singing and the tenor playing Faust dropping straight down through a trapdoor).

The moral of this story is: Even if you believe in the Devil (and Witches don't), you probably should get a good lawyer to read over your contract. Personally, I'd never do business with any guy holding a pitchfork.

Our Award for the Most Disgusting Love Spell in History

It was a tough choice, given that spell from Marie Laveau, but the winner's got to be the ancient love potion made from bugs. And here it is, straight from the work of the legendary Albertus Magnus, just as he wrote it, with my notes:

> Take of pismires or ants (the biggest, having the sourest smell are the best) two handfuls; spirits of wine, one gallon; digest them in a glass vessel, close shut, for the space of a month, in which time they will be dissolved in a liquor, then distill them in balneo [*ya got me!*] til all be dry. Then put in the same quantity of ants as before; do this three times, then aromatize the spirit with cinnamon. [*Oh yeah, like the cinnamon is gonna be a big help.*]

But don't despair if this sounds too vomit-making for you. Albertus has an alternate recipe! To the same basic mixture, he added two hundred wood lice and two hundred fifty bees for more potency. Yum! Part of this complete breakfast! I guess the wood lice are in there for extra fiber. This love potion might work, but I doubt that any woman or man is going to be in a romantic mood after spending the evening ralphing into the porcelain throne.

Okay, You *Can* Try These at Home: Talismans, Amulets, and Charms

Talismans and amulets are often considered the same thing, but they're not. The difference is that talismans carry their own supernatural power, which is then transferred to the maker or owner of the talisman; amulets are used to ward off evil. Amulets these days are more loosely defined to include any magic charms for any purpose.

A Witch's Cord would be an amulet, of sorts, but a rose quartz crystal would be a talisman, since the stone itself carries its own power.

Talismans

The older and more traditional form of talismans are magical words or symbols written on paper, carved on gemstones, or engraved on metal disks.

Elsewhere in this book, we've made talismans of dripped wax from magically charged candles, with magical signs "engraved" in the wax. These are valid talismans because the colored wax carries its own magic, and the mystical signs were written on the talisman by the magician making it (you, in case you hadn't noticed).

Talismans are traditionally written on "virgin parchment" which is going to be pretty hard to find, since real parchment isn't sold at your local Office Max. But parchment-type paper is popular these days. As to whether it's a virgin or not, let's assume yes. (Actually, that means that nothing has ever been written on it—which lets out recycled—and it has no watermark.)

Also, it helps to enchant the ink you're going to write it with. This isn't too tough: Just charge the ink and/or the pen for your magical purpose.

Written Talismans

One of the most potent written talismans is the Abracadabra talisman, which is used elsewhere in this book. Another famous one is the *Sator* talisman, written like this:

```
S A T O R
A R E P O
T E N E T
O P E R A
R O T A S
```

This is known as a letter square, since the letters spell the same words vertically and horizontally, upward, backward, downward, or from the right or left.

This particular Sator talisman was originally used for putting out fires. As late as 1742, people in Saxony had special wooden plates bearing the Sator square ready to toss into a house fire to extinguish it. The Latin translation is roughly "Arepo, the Sower, holds back the works with his wheels." Even translated, it's still in question, since no one has been able to assign a meaning to the word "Arepo." The thing about ceremonial magic is that you have to take quite a lot of it on faith . . . and with a grain of salt.

You'd use this talisman by writing your spell for love, a happy marriage, healing conflict between lovers, whatever, on the paper, then writing the talisman.

The talisman can be carried, hung on a Witch's Cord, added to a Conjure Bag, or burned in a Fire Spell.

A version of this is for gaining the love of a woman, and is attributed to the mage Abremalin, sometimes called Abraham the Jew. It dates from 1458. Just remember to word your spell in such a way that it is not manipulative. These written talismans are old and powerful, and you don't want that power turning on you.

```
S A L O M
A R E P O
L E M E L
O P E R A
M O L A S
```

♥ *Pentagram Love Spell*

The pentagram is an ancient magical symbol that has been adopted by modern Witches as the symbol of our religion. A five-pointed star surrounded by a circle, the points stand for the four elements of earth, air, fire, and water which make up all life. At the top is Spirit, the animating force of life. The circle represents the cycle of life, death, and rebirth, with no beginning or ending. It's also an old symbol of magical protection. Witches usually do our magic inside the protection of a circle that has been cleared of harmful energies, usually by burning frankincense and myrrh inside the circle's perimeter.

The pentagram itself is a potent magical force, but combined with the forces of the four elements and of spirit, it makes a powerful ritual for love or anything else. This spell will be done over the course of five nights. Or days. Actually, there's no reason you can't do it during the daytime, I just prefer working at night when it's quieter. Just try to do it at the same time each day, but don't worry if you can't.

You'll need:

Five votive candles: white, red, blue, green, and yellow
Holder for the candles, either clear glass or tinted in the
    colors of the candles
Paper large enough to draw a pentagram of at least a ten to
    twelve inches in diameter
Red pen, marker, or crayon to draw the pentagram
Parchment paper and a red pen to write the spell

Draw the pentagram as in the illustration, in red. When you draw the star, draw it using one unbroken line, never lifting the pen from the paper. Don't worry if the circle is a little lopsided or the star is uneven, but do the best you can.

Place the votive candleholders at each point of the star. Don't put the candles in yet.

Hold each of the candles between your hands, one at a time, and charge the candle with the proper incantation. Insert the candle in the holder, light it, and go on the next one. Start at the top of the Pentacle with the white candle and work clockwise.

[White candle] *I charge you with the life of the spirit, that my spirit may be enriched by love, both giving and receiving it*

[Blue candle] *I charge you with the power of water, for healing power of love, understanding, and compassion*
[Red candle] *I charge you with the power of fire, for love's passion*
[Green candle] *I charge you with the power of earth, for stability and steadfastness in love*
[Yellow candle] *I charge you with the power of air, for the intuitive, imaginative power of love*

On the parchment, and in red ink, write your name and the following spell:

Spirits of earth, air, fire, and water, crowned by spirit of Universal Love, I call upon you to bring me my true, perfect lover. By your power, we will be lovers and friends to each other, sharing our happiness with the world around us. This spell is done with harm to none.

Read the spell aloud, and place it in the center of the penta-gram. If you need to fold it, that's fine.

Let the candles burn while you close your eyes and concen-trate on the joys of love, what love means to you, what you can offer a lover as well as what a lover can offer you. You don't need to take a lot of time with this, but do give it some thought. Don't try to picture a specific person: that limits your options.

For the next four nights, repeat the incantations as you light the candles, and read your spell again each night. On the first night, start with Water, the second with Fire, the third with Earth, and the fourth with Air. In other words, you're starting with a different element each time. After you've finished the en-tire spell on the last night, keep the written spell in a safe place until your love comes along. Then the spell has done its work, so burn it. When you do, say the following:

Powers of Earth, Air, Fire, and Water, power of Spirit, thank you for your help, and go on your way with my thanks.

8

Anti-Love Spells:
Taking the Off Ramp on the
Highway of Love

Free at last, free at last! Oh, praise Jesus, I'm free at last!
— Martin Luther King

We thought it was going to be forever, we thought it was going to be wine and roses and everlasting kisses under the summer lantern lights.

Yeah, well, we were *wrong*.

The eternal flame of your passion died down like a backyard barbecue in a rainstorm, and now you just can't wait to get rid of that jerk.

Or maybe you've already broken up, and what you need is closure to get rid of the last of those feelings and move on. Or you weren't ready to break up, but the other person was, and now here you are, still in love and miserable.

This is no way to live.

As the saying has it, "living well is the best revenge." There's nothing that pisses off an old lover more than the fact that you're not home shedding tears and living with your memories. You don't have to jump into another relationship right away—

in fact, it's a lot better if you don't—but you do have to find interesting, engrossing things to do with your life. You probably
have interesting things to do already, things you didn't have time
for when you were making time for a lover.

Now, let's say you're the dumper rather than the dumpee.
Okay, the relationship is not working and you want out. Try a
few spells for understanding and gentleness before you break
the bad news. And don't think that the old "I hope we can still
be friends" line is going to work—that's impossible, for now.
Just make a nice, clean break so both of you can start again. You
can be friends later, but for now, why pick at scabs? Let it heal.

Actually, one of the wickedest breaking-up lines I ever heard
involved that "let's be friends" line. My friend was involved with
a guy who considered himself quite a stud. Every time he broke
up with a woman he said the same thing, "I still want to be your
friend, but I just don't want to go to bed with you anymore."
She sort of looked at him, trying not to laugh, and said, "Oh
gosh, that's too bad. I have enough friends. The only use I could
possibly have for you would be to _____ you." (Fornicatory
expletive deleted, but I'm sure you can figure it out.)

He never forgave her for not falling for his best manipulative
move, and everyone who heard the story just cracked up. Especially his exes.

Sometimes, like the song says, *love stinks*. And when it does,
your best air freshener is magic.

♥   The Prick Spell

For this one, you'll need a black balloon.

Write the person's name in black ink on a piece of white
paper, and the phrase *"I no longer love you."*

Stick the paper in a balloon and blow up the balloon. Then
prick the balloon with a pin and throw the entire thing in the
garbage, feeling the last bit of affection for this person explode

into tiny bits. This is where the spell gets its name. Why? What did you think?

♥ Rotten-to-the-Core Spell

Take an apple, the symbol of love, and core it. Into the hole where the core was, place this spell written in black ink:

I banish the romantic love I felt for [name]. *As this apple withers, so do my feelings for him/her wither.*

Then bury the apple.

♥ Kiss-Off of the Spider Woman

The terrible thing about emotional entanglements is that they're just so complex that sorting them out is like trying to unravel a spider web. This is a spell to unbind yourself from the emotional web that entangles you in old relationships.

For this spell you need a pen, paper, and a lot of string.

Find a place where you can be alone and think. Turn off the phone, turn off the TV and the music.

Sit alone for a while and think about the aspects of your relationship. In the middle of the paper, draw a small circle, and in the circle put the names of you and your lover. Then, in smaller circles, but connected by straight lines to the middle one, write all the emotions connected with the relationship: love, loss, betrayal, happiness, misery . . . whatever. If you want to get specific, by all means let it out on the paper. Just scrawl whatever comes into your mind. But connect everything, like a spider's web. Emotions and relationships are like that: interconnected and messy.

Then crumple up the paper into a ball. Start wrapping the string around it, and as you wrap it, don't censor your emotions: You feel what you feel.

When you've got it really wrapped up, just sit for a minute with the balled-up paper in your hands and say this charm:

These are the emotions, the problems, the good times and the bad times of this relationship. But they're over, they're in the past, they can no longer entangle me and strangle me, they can no longer hold me back from living and growing. As I unwrap this string, so am I untangled from these emotions, I am cut free of them.

Now start unwrapping the string from the ball. As you do it, feel all the bonds and tangled web of emotions fall away from you, setting you free. You no longer need them.

When the paper is unwrapped, don't bother to uncrumple it. Dump it in the garbage, along with the rest of the junk you don't need anymore.

♥ *Sail Away Spell*

Take a leaf, a real one. Write on the leaf the name of the person you're breaking up with, and sail it out on a large body of water. The spell is:

I break the power of this person over me. As this leaf sails away, so do my feelings for him/her.

As you watch the leaf sail away, take a deep breath and let it out slowly. As you do, feel all the old emotions begin to let go and drift off.

♥ *Disgusting, but Fun, Banishing Spell*

I like this spell a lot. Not only is it simple and effective, but it gives you a great feeling of personal satisfaction. Use it if someone's done you dirty in love.

Take a piece of toilet paper (I'm sure you can see where this is going).
Write the person's name on it nine times in black ink.
When the time comes, use the toilet paper.
As you flush, repeat the following ancient incantation: "We're *through*, jerk!"

I'm sure you can come up with your own name for this spell. I'd tell you mine but this is a family-type book.

Someone told me a version of this spell where you put the paper in the bottom of the cat box and leave it there. For a long, *long* time. Nice kitty!

♥ *Sever the "Ties That Bind" Spell*

Each time we begin a new relationship, we do so with the greatest of hopes and expectations for the future. Unfortunately not all of the relationships work out as we plan. And regardless of how friendly or not so friendly the relationship ends, it may be necessary to formally, and magically, cut any emotional or spiritual bonds that formed over the course of time. Only by doing this can we hope to reduce our chances of dragging the baggage of an old relationship into the start of a new one. This spell should be done on a Saturday during the waning of the moon, if possible, for greatest potency.

> One black candle, to symbolize the "death" or end of the old relationship
> One white candle, to symbolize freshness and new beginnings
> Fluorite-chip necklace, to help calm the emotions of those involved
> Clear quartz-chip necklace, to help rebalance and redirect the energies
> Frankincense and myrrh incense, for cleansing and purification
> At least three feet of red thread and a pair of scissors

Inscribe the black candle with the following runes:

EIHWAZ   NIED   FEHU

Eihwaz: to banish any potential stumbling blocks that may
   impede one's future growth.
Nied: to banish feelings of distress over the loss of a relationship
Fehu: to move events smoothly forward to their next stage

Hold the black candle firmly in both hands and pour into it
all the sadness, anger, despair, and hurt feelings you may still
have about the relationship. If you feel comfortable, you may
want to speak these feelings out loud to put that extra "umph"
into it. When you are finished, put the candle back into its
holder and encircle it with the fluorite. Next inscribe the white
candle with the following runes:

DAEG   EOLH   KENAZ

Daeg: to help develop a new, healthy attitude
Eolh: to help rebuild and strengthen the life-force
Kenaz: to promote emotional healing and spiritual well-being.

Hold the white candle firmly in both hands and pour into
this candle all your hopes for the future. See yourself happy, vig-
orous, and enthusiastic for life. Again, if you wish, you may
speak these thoughts aloud to give things a little extra juice.
When finished, put the candle back in its holder and place at
least nine inches from the black candle. Encircle the white candle with the quartz necklace.

Tie a loop of red thread to the black candle to anchor it, and
then string the two candles together so that there are three separate lines connecting the black and white candles. These are the
"ties that bind." Say out loud:

*As red is the color of life, this red thread binds these two candles
together, making them as one. As these candles are joined, so too,
were* [name of other person] *and I joined as one. As these threads
are severed, so are the bonds that join* [name] *and me severed.*

Pick up the scissors and cut the first strand and say:

With conviction and malice toward none, I sever the ties of the mind that exist between us.

Cut the second strand and say:

With conviction and malice toward none, I sever the ties of the heart that exist between us.

Cut the third and final strand and say:

With conviction and malice toward none, I sever the ties of the spirit that exist between us.

As these candles, once joined as one, have now again become two, so it now is with [name] and me. From this point froward, with conviction and malice to none, I am separate, complete and whole. Gone forever are the ties that bind!

After the candles have burned themselves out, take the thread and any remains of the black candle as far away from your home as is reasonable (preferably to someplace you would never otherwise go) and bury them, not looking back as you leave. You may also wish to bury the fluorite necklace as well. Or, should you decide to keep the fluorite, be sure to cleanse it by soaking it in salt water for two or three days, then recharge it for positive results before you use it again. Wrap the remains of the white candle in a white cotton hand-kerchief and keep it in a safe place as a talisman for hope and success. Wear the quartz necklace for at least three days following the ritual, or anytime you need a little "boost" of self-confidence.

♥ *Solitary Pleasures Spell*

This doesn't mean what you think it means.

Well, maybe it *could* mean that, but you'd need a few more items, batteries not included.

But this is a spell to remind you that being alone is not necessarily a bad thing, that you're accountable to no one else for your time, and that you can do what you want to do without having to consider what another person wants.

But some people are absolutely terrified of doing anything alone. They can't conceive of going to the movies or the theater alone, and the idea of sitting alone in a nice restaurant is unthinkable. They feel as if everyone will notice they're alone and feel sorry for them, or figure they just couldn't get a date.

But you know . . . nobody cares. They probably don't even notice, they're so busy with their own problems or circumstances. And these days, with so many executives of both sexes traveling alone, no one thinks anything of it when she sees someone sitting at a table for one. In fact, someone sitting at a table for two, but in a bad relationship, is probably envying you.

There's a big difference between being lonely and being alone, and that difference is solely a state of mind. Being lonely is being a victim; being alone is enjoying your own company.

Here's a Scented Fire Spell for getting back in touch with the good things you like to do. Review the general rules on Scented Fire in chapter 1.

You'll need:

A metal bowl and something heatproof to set it on
91 percent rubbing alcohol (or regular rubbing alcohol if you
    can't get 91 percent)
Essential oil: any scent that you particularly like and that
    makes you feel good. I like orange: it's always cheerful.

Sit in a comfortable position, in a room with the lights low, not in the dark (you'll need to see to light the fire in the bowl) with the Scented Fire bowl in front of you. Some people like to sit in a lotus position on the floor, some feel more comfortable in a chair.

Light the fire and watch it burn. As you watch, let yourself think about all the things you like to do, and which you can now do all by yourself. If feelings of fear or nervousness come up, face them and say:

Okay, I'm not going to be afraid. I'm not letting this stop me. I'm stronger than that.

See yourself enjoying a meal alone, enjoying a show, going to a concert or a museum. Really feel the pleasure in doing these things without having to worry about what someone else thinks.

When the fire dies down, let yourself relax and remember the nice, warm freedom of doing what you want, when you want.

♥   The Love Exorcist

Witches believe that everything that happens in a house or in a particular space leaves its own vibrations, its own atmosphere.

When you've broken up with someone, you need to get rid of all the spiritual, emotional, and supernatural baggage that still lingers in the space you shared. This is the same incense we use when exorcising unwanted spirits from a haunted house. Only the ritual is a little different.

Incense: Frankincense and myrrh in equal amounts, about a tablespoon of each. Frankincense and myrrh are resins, and burn better in that state, but you can get them powdered. They work almost as well. Since ancient times, the combination of frankincense and myrrh has been used to drive out evil spirits and purify an area, especially before religious rituals. The Catholic church still uses this dynamite combination as church incense. Witches use it too. One of the few things we agree on.

For this, you're going to need your charcoal burning in a sand-filled bowl, so that it doesn't get too hot, because you're going to be carrying it from room to room. Use potholders and both hands—you don't want to drop this stuff! When the charcoal is going good, spoon in a heaping amount of the incense;

this is going to get *very* smoky, so take care of the smoke alarms (be sure to turn them back on immediately after the ritual)!

Carry the incense around the house. Get the smoke going around the perimeter of each room, into the four corners, into closets, in the bathroom—everywhere. When the smoke dies down, throw more incense on the charcoal. As you're purifying the area, say:

I drive out all the influences and disruptive emotions associated with [name of the recently ousted]. I purify this area of all vibrations and energies associated with him/her."

Repeat this in every room. You should feel the atmosphere lighten up.

♥ *Ancient Spell for Diminishing*

This is very old magic, the most famous of all spells to cause things to die away. If you're dealing with your own pain, your leftover emotions, or the kind of anger and sorrow that follow a breakup, this is an extremely powerful spell to get rid of those harmful feelings.

No one can say exactly where this spell came from, and it's mystified almost every scholar who has tried to find its meaning. The best guess is that it was originally from the Chaldean and meant "Perish like the word." It may have been a spell to banish fever, which would make it effective against the fevers of love. It's too bad that this word, which is so powerful as a talisman, should have been taken over by stage magicians and used as a joke.

Used properly, it's no joke.

The spell must be written and spoken, with a space for silence at the end. After it's finished, you wear the spell as a talisman, next to your body and touching your skin, as long as you think you need it.

On a piece of white paper, with black ink, write:

As this word diminishes, so do all my feelings of love, anger, hurt, and pain connected with [name of person] diminish and vanish. This spell is done with harm to none.

ABRACADABRA
ABRACADABR
ABRACADAB
ABRACADA
ABRACAD
ABRACA
ABRAC
ABRA
ABR
AB
A

♥ *When You're Ready to Start Over . . .*
The Simplest Love Spell of All

Another wonderful spell from Jane Raeburn. Jane performed this spell for herself and the results have been gratifying in *every* sense of the word! You'll need:

A red votive candle and a votive candleholder
Patchouli oil, cinnamon oil, rose oil, or all three

This is for when you're ready for a new partner. First, make sure you're really ready, that you've gotten over the hurts of the past and are ready to give to a new person.

Anoint the red candle with patchouli (for a sensuous lover), cinnamon (for an affectionate, balanced relationship) or rose (for abiding love). Hold it in your hands and close your eyes as you enter a meditative state.

When you are connected with your Higher Self, begin visualizing yourself having a wonderful time with someone new. Don't imagine any details about this person, you don't want to close off any possibilities, or you might miss out on someone wonderful! Instead, see yourself doing the things you would do with a partner—walking, dining, playing sports, going to cultural events, worshipping, shopping, snuggling, reading, making love. See yourself having a FABULOUS time with this person, giving and receiving.

Say these words:

I open my heart to a new love. I open my mind to a new love. I open my soul to a new love.

Pray to the deity of your choice:

Venus [or God or Allah or Mother Earth], *help me to be truly open to a new love. Help me to be the best person I can be, so that I may be deserving of such a love.*

Describe the sort of love you seek, being careful to describe a relationship rather than a person.

I place this quest in Your hands, and trust you to bring it to fruition with harm to none and in keeping with my fate.

As you say this last sentence, reach forward and put the candle in the votive candleholder and put it down on a table, altar, or shelf. As you make this gesture, mentally place your search in the deity's keeping. Light the candle and let it burn all night in a safe place, away from kids or pets. When you awake, know that your deity is looking after your search for love. Concentrate on doing the things that renew and awaken you. Take up a new creative project, finish an old one, cut out a bad habit, see the friends who leave you energized, limit your time with the people who drain you. Challenge yourself to be an interesting, confident, thoughtful person. Know that love will follow.

9

The Myths and the Truth
of Today's Witches:
Step Back, Margaret Hamilton!

When some people find out I'm a Witch and that I live in Salem, the first question they ask (I mean the first question beyond, "Ya got any love spells?") is, "Why would a Witch want to live where witches were hanged?"

Interesting question. First of all, lots of Witches live in Salem. There are so many of us that no one blinks an eye when we do outdoor rituals or when we go out on the street wearing full Witchy regalia on our way to celebrate our sacred days. Salem is a city very aware of a past in which innocent people were murdered in the name of Witchcraft, and are determined never to repeat it. Like most small towns in New England, many of the descendants of the original settlers still live here; in today's Salem descendants of persecutor and persecuted live side by side, the past not forgotten but forgiven.

Every time I hear about Witches in other places around the country being persecuted, ridiculed, and even physically attacked because of their religion—and I hear about it a lot—I count myself lucky to live in Salem. Many Witches in other places can't even wear the pentagram, the symbol of our religion, although their coworkers are allowed to wear their crosses.

Salem is a beautiful town. The architectural styles range from early Colonial saltboxes to elegant Federals and whimsical Victorians, and walking down most of our streets is like walking into history. The great part about visiting friends in a town like this is that they all live in such interesting houses.

Some of the Witches who live in Salem were born here. Most of us started out as tourists and liked the city enough to move here. Some of us have jobs in Boston and prefer to live away from the inconvenience of the city.

In October, Salem turns into Halloween Central, with thousands of visitors crowding the streets and dozens of "haunted" tourist attractions opening up all over town, and the city staging a month-long party called Haunted Happenings. No matter how crazy it gets here for that month, and it gets plenty hysterical, we like it here.

WEB of Salem, a Witches' educational and community service group, has informational brochures that they give to tourists, and these explain modern and historical Witchcraft in a simple question-and-answer format. So, with WEB's permission, I'm reprinting one of their brochures here.

QUESTIONS AND ANSWERS ABOUT WITCHES, WICCANS, AND PAGANS

The main thing to remember about Witchcraft is that it is a very personal religion without an all-encompassing dogma and with no established authorities like bishops or popes. Because of this, it is impossible to say that all Witches believe the same things or that one person is a "leader" of the Witches. Witches are usually organized into covens, each coven with a priestess or priest or both, and the coven establishes its own rules of religious practice.

To add to the confusion, many Witches practice as *solitaries,* preferring to develop their own spiritual path in their own way.

There are some general ethical and religious guidelines accepted by most Witches, and those guidelines are established by the religious practice called *Wicca*. Wicca is what we'll be talking about here.

Wicca is the best-known branch of the religion of the Witches, and was established as a legal religion by a 1986 Federal court decision. It's a modern interpretation of ancient Pagan religion, centering around the worship of a Goddess *and* a God, united in a universal deity. Although Wiccans honor many Gods and Goddesses, we believe that they are all aspects of the One. Our deities include the gods of ancient Rome, Greece, and Egypt, the Celtic tribal gods, the Norse gods, and many more from various cultures. Wicca is primarily an earth religion: we believe that every living thing is an aspect of our Earth Goddess, and is to be treated with respect. Most Wiccans also call themselves Witches, and there are many denominations, or "Traditions" within Wicca.

We believe in reincarnation, in the cycle of birth, death, and rebirth. We have no concepts of "sin," "heaven," or "hell." We believe that each Witch carries the responsibility to make his or her life fruitful and happy, and to give that happiness back to the world by doing good wherever possible.

Are there "black" and "white" Witches?

No. The basic law of Wicca states "Do as you will and harm no living thing." The second part of that law is, "everything you do comes back to you threefold." No real Witch would ever consider doing harm: it's against our religion. People who do harm, no matter what they say, are *not witches.*

Do Witches worship the Devil?

No. We don't believe in the "Devil" or "Satan." Satan is a Christian concept and Witchcraft is not a Christian-based religion. The confusion probably arose because of our "Horned God." The Horned God (sometimes identified as Pan or the Roman/Celtic Cernunnos) was the god of the hunt. He was depicted as having antlers and was identified with the animals he provided as food for our Pagan ancestors. Without his help in making the hunt successful, our ancestors would have starved in the winter, when there were no crops.

Is Witchcraft a "women's religion?"

Not at all. It's true that Witchcraft is a very liberating religion for women, since it's Goddess-centered, but because we hold our God in equal importance, it's also liberating for men. Witches believe that everything in nature has a male and a female side; we also believe that without the equal balance of male and female in nature, nothing can have life. We truly believe that man and woman were created equal, and hold no one sex dominant over the other. We believe that sexuality is a private issue, and do not condemn homosexuals.

A male Witch is called a Witch. "Warlock" is an old Scottish term and means "oathbreaker" or "traitor."

Why do Witches wear black?

We don't always wear black. You usually see us wearing black or black robes in October because it's the Feast of Samhain, a time for us to honor our dead, and black is associated with that day. Black has always been the color of the clergy, and many Wiccan clergy wear it while serving in an official capacity. However, most Witches don't wear black or robes all the time, just as a priest or pastor doesn't wear full vestments all the time. We have jobs and lives and wear what everyone else wears.

Does Witchcraft involve any "sacrifice"?

Never. Our Goddess and God do not require any human or animal sacrifice, no matter what you see in the horror movies. The very idea of harming a living thing is repulsive to Witches, so much so that many of us are vegetarians.

Do our rites involve children?

Not usually. We have a rite called "Wiccaning" which is much like a Christian christening. It's performed for children at the parent's request and is intended, not to make the child a Witch or bind the child in any way to our religion, but merely to give the child the protection of the Goddess until the child is old enough to make his/her own religious decisions.

With all the negative associations, why do we still use the term "Witch"?

The word "Witch" has been much abused through the ages. It is our aim to correct the lies that have gone unchallenged since

the Dark Ages, and that have resulted in the persecution and dis-
crimination that still continues today. We aren't asking people to
"convert" or even to agree with us, but we *are* insisting on the dig-
nity due any ethical religion that is faithfully held. It is our hope that,
as more Witches speak out, the word "Witch" will begin to lose
those undeserved associations.

Why Witches Hate Walt Disney

It's not so much old Uncle Walt—it's the Disney movies with the
terrible images of Witches as ugly and evil that piss us off. But,
to be fair, Disney had nothing to do with *The Wizard of Oz,* in
which Margaret Hamilton, playing the Wicked Witch of the
West, set the prevailing image of a Witch as a wicked, green-
faced hag. Why the green face is anybody's guess. When someone mentions Witches, it's never Glinda the Good with that
glittery dress and the bubble limo that people think of; it's Mean
Ol' Maggie zooming overhead on that broom like Chuck Yeager
breaking the sound barrier, tossing fireballs, and cackling, ". . .
and your little dog, too!"

Three hundred years of the Inquisition, and we needed *this?*

Then came *Rosemary's Baby,* which took a bunch of baby-
stealing Devil-worshippers and called them Witches. This kind
of stereotype came from the days of the Inquisition. In 1468, a
pair of fanatical Dominican monks named Kramer and Sprenger
wrote the guidelines for sniffing out who was a Witch. Those
guidelines included such disgusting practices as human sacrifice,
drinking blood, stealing babies, kissing parts of anatomy not
normally used for this purpose, and some other vomit-inducing
stuff, quite a lot of it sexual, painful-sounding, and kinky. Makes
you wonder whether celibacy was really a good idea for those
two. Talk about guys who *needed* to get laid!

But Kramer and Sprenger said that all this was because
of the Devil, whom they actually believed in. (Funny that
Witches don't believe in the Devil, but religious fanatics seem to
think about him all the time!) And the book they wrote,

the *Malleus Maleficarum,* became the handbook for finding out who was a Witch, what kind of torture to apply to get a confession, what the confession should say (the monks wrote it—all you had to do was sign your name, just like buying a house through a really bad lawyer) and how it didn't make any difference if the accused insisted they were innocent because, by God, they were *guilty!* This book formed the image of Witches that still persists today, the proof that a good lie never dies, provided you can get enough suckers to believe it.

Two hundred years after the *Malleus Maleficarum* was written, its basic philosophy jumped the ocean and settled in for a season in the Massachusetts Bay Colony, in 1692.

The History of Witches in Salem

A lot of visitors to Salem wonder what the infamous Salem Witch trials have to do with contemporary Witches.

Actually, nothing.

To understand the Salem Witch trials, it's important to understand what Salem was like. It had an economy based on farming, and the residents lived under constant threat of death from the Native Americans. Not that the Native Americans weren't justified in trying to hold off their own overthrow, but still, it was a bad time. The Puritans who settled here were not warriors. They were just farmers.

To say that times were tough isn't saying nearly enough. It's hard for Americans like us to imagine what it was like to starve to death, to watch our families starve. We see news reports about "war-torn" nations whose people are dying from starvation, but we can't really understand the terror involved. When all you have to live on are your crops, and your fields are being torn apart by armies and bombs, or you can't tend the crops because half the family is out fighting and the other half is too young to work the fields, then things get desperate.

The people of the Massachusetts Bay Colony, and especially the people in Salem Village, the farming part of Salem, lived under this threat all the time. Many of them had seen friends and family killed in Indian raids. And you have to remember the Puritan mindset. They called themselves "the Saints," they were convinced that they were God's anointed, and they couldn't figure out why God would let bad things happen to them.

The only answer—for some of them, a very convenient answer—was that they had offended God in some way. And, thanks to good King James and men like him, they knew what that way was: Evidently someone among them had offended God by consorting with the Devil. Witchcraft.

The idea of Witchcraft may have been dying out in Europe, under the coming ideas of the Enlightenment, but these were the Colonies, at the ends of the earth. New ideas were slow in taking hold here.

So that idea was in the back of many people's minds. Add to that the old feuds, bad blood between families, a mistrust of independent women, and prime property held by rivals. And the peculiar sense of self-righteousness held by the Puritans. Plus, Salem Village (now the town of Danvers) and Salem Town (now modern-day Salem) had conflicts. Salem Village was a farming economy, with the houses spaced far apart and more vulnerable to attack. Salem Town was a seaport, more cosmopolitan, harder to attack. And there had been ongoing arguments over the appointment of Rev. Samuel Parris as the pastor of the Salem Village church. Lots of people didn't like him, and the battle lines were drawn along the same lines as the old family rivalries. It didn't help that Parris himself was a stubborn, confrontational man who thrived on controversy.

All it took was an incident to set if off.

The incident occurred in Parris's own house. His nine-year-old daughter, Betty, and his twelve-year-old niece, Abigail Williams (who had seen her parents killed in an Indian massacre), were playing fortune-telling games with the family slave, a West Indian woman named Tituba. Of course, fortune-telling was forbidden, but it was, oddly enough, a common pastime in the colony. Pretty soon, the two girls invited other girls to take part, among them Ann Putnam and Mercy Lewis.

Nobody knows exactly why, but little Betty started having nightmares and screaming fits. She was the youngest, and she had most likely been frightened by the older girls. Parris and his wife couldn't figure out what was wrong with her, and neither could the village doctor. When Abigail and the others saw the attention Betty was getting, suddenly they went into "fits" too. The doctor, having absolutely no idea what the problem was, came up with a last resort: The girls, he said were "under an evil hand." In other words, bewitched.

This started a few people thinking. If the girls were bewitched, then some among them were Witches. And who better to accuse than those people who had disagreed with Reverend Parris and the town political faction that supported him?

At first the girls didn't have an answer when the older people started pushing them to say exactly who had done this to them. But young Ann Putnam had a very vengeful mother, also named Ann, whose family had some long-standing grudges. It was the adults who first suggested names to the children.

The first names that the children screamed out were women who were of no real importance, but who were town annoyances: the beggar Sarah Good and old Sarah Osborne. Sarah Osborne had scandalized the town when she was younger by marrying her indentured servant. Sarah Good was of a prominent family, but she had lost all her money and property and was now an embarrassing reminder of what could happen with one crop failure. Arrested along with Good, who was pregnant, was her daughter, Dorcas, four years old.

The real test came with the accusation of Rebecca Nurse. Rebecca's Puritan credentials were impeccable. She and her husband were staunch church members and well-to-do-farmers. But

Rebecca's family had had a long feud with Ann Putnam's. If the accusers could get away with convicting Rebecca, then nothing could stop them.

Rebecca, in her late seventies and bedridden, was hauled out of her house, taken to jail, and strip-searched in an attempt to find "Witch marks," any mole, growth of skin, or discoloration on the body that proved you were a Witch. Frequently, said the *Malleus Maleficarum,* these were concealed on the Witch's private parts.

It's absolutely incomprehensible to us to realize how terribly modest the Puritan women were. And for a sick, pious old lady, it must have been a special kind of torture. Besides, at her age, who doesn't have some kind of mark?

Rebecca was acquitted. But the girls, who were now being referred to as "the afflicted," staged even more spectacular fits in court, saying that Rebecca had come to them in the night and hurt them. When the judges asked how she could have done that, since she had been in jail, the girls said that Rebecca's specter had done it.

This cleared the ground for the most heinous technique of the trials: spectral evidence. The idea that you could be two places at once.

Rebecca's jury was told to go back and think again. They did, returning with a guilty verdict. Both of her sisters were also arrested. Only one escaped hanging.

This kind of thing went on until there were 150 people in jail; nineteen were hanged, one was pressed to death with rocks for refusing to enter a plea, and five people died in jail, including old Sarah Osborne and the newborn infant of Sarah Good. Little Dorcas Good was finally released, after being chained in irons most of the time and having confessed to being a Witch, but she was mentally ill all her life. An interesting side note: the last group of "Witches" were hanged on September 21, the Autumn Equinox, an important date in the Wiccan year.

With so many people in jail, the economy of Salem Village collapsed. No one could properly tend the farms. It was years before the town recovered.

There were never any real Witches in Salem in 1692. This was a Puritan colony, remember. The Puritan definition of a Witch was someone who had dealings with Satan and placed curses and hexes on people.

There is no connection with modern-day Witches and the accused Witches of 1692. They were ordinary people accused of awful crimes. Their deaths and imprisonment served political, social, and economic ends. They have nothing in common with the Witches of today, except that we sympathize with their persecution and feel great sadness for the injustices against them. They were not real Witches. But they were courageous innocents.

Witchcraft today is a revival of old Pagan religions centering around respect for the earth and the worship of God as a dual deity, both male and female, with the Goddess as the original creator of all. Today's Witches belong to a religion whose roots are older than Christianity; they do not believe in Satan or a devil. Satan is an invention of Christianity in the Middle Ages: The Devil gave the church a tool with which to rid itself of heretics.

So Ya Wanna Be a Witch?

It isn't that hard, but it isn't that easy.

And there you have it, the paradox of modern Paganism.

Actually, it's making the actual decision that's the hard part. How do you know that a religion or a particular set of beliefs is right for you? Especially a religion that's so fraught with supposed mystery and mystical folklore and flat-out bad press?

You don't. Not just off the bat.

But if you're interested, and you ask questions, and the answers seem good for you, then the decision is yours. Witches and Pagans don't proselytize; we aren't out there beating the bushes for converts. We'd rather not have anyone be *persuaded* to join us; we'd rather let the Goddess and God whisper in someone's ear.

There are no set-in-stone rituals, no secret handshakes, no official spells. The way you honor your Goddess and God is up to you. (I practice Roman Paganism, and incorporate the religious beliefs of ancient Rome into Wicca. And not just because the Romans had more holidays than there were days in the calendar and that many of them involved wine and a really nice buffet. No sirree!)

The best way to find out more on Wicca and Witchcraft is to read. Read a *lot*. I've listed a few beginner's books for you, but you should read everything you can get your hands on, because all of it is merely *opinion*. There is not one religion in the world, not Christianity, not Judaism, not Hinduism—nothing—that is not opinion, no matter how many people share that opinion and how many learned and "holy" books have been written on the subject. Every holy book was written by someone who claimed that God told 'em what to say. Religion is manmade; it's our way of working with the natural world and the invisible world. We even make up our deities, giving names and attributes to forces that we don't understand, in an attempt to make them more comprehensible to us.

The forces are real; our way of working with those forces is artificial, even though it works. One man hears the word of God. I hear the word of Diana and Apollo. Conventional wisdom today says that my god is false, but two thousand years ago, today's god was false and mine was accepted as one of the true gods. Who's right? We both are.

Not that that makes religion any less real to us. Religion can be our guide, our comfort, something to cling to in times of trouble and doubt, something to help us celebrate in times of joy. It's our very real link to the invisible world.

If your religion isn't giving you that kind of satisfaction, then you shouldn't be practicing it, no matter whether it's Wicca, Catholicism, Voodoo, or anything else. It's too personal a choice to let someone else make for you.

This is why it infuriates me that some people try to "convert" other people. How can you possibly declare one religion wrong and another right?: It's all choice and emotion.

If you want to study Wicca, I would warn you strongly against looking for a teacher or a coven right away. Because of the "mystique" surrounding Witchcraft, we now have just as many crazies and fakes as the Christians have to put up with. Anyone can set him or herself up as an authority with plenty of "credentials" to prove it. But remember that we have no authorities. The best way to find a good teacher is to read a lot, ask a lot of questions of a potential teacher, and remember that no one is infallible. The most effective way to be a Witch is to talk and share ideas with other Witches. This is why forming study groups with other people who are interested is such a good idea. These usually morph into covens.

Covens are groups of people who have decided to practice in a certain way. Many of them teach their own methods of religious practice. This is logical: if you wanted to be a Methodist, you wouldn't go ask the local rabbi to teach you. If you join a coven, you agree to abide by its form of practice. If you don't, don't join. Find another group, or start your own. That's perfectly valid.

One thing you'll never encounter among real Wiccans is sex as a requirement for coven membership, initiation, instruction, or for any other reason. Avoid anyone who tells you that you have to have sex with somebody to join the group or to advance to the next level. Also avoid any person or group who insists on secrecy because they have "so much power that they have enemies." That's a crock.

Ritual nudity is an issue. Some groups do indeed practice "skyclad" as they call it, feeling that in a nature religion, you should be as nature made you. These groups are becoming very rare because of the potential for abuse of the nudity. And that abuse usually comes from people who join, hoping for some kind of sexual thrill or because they've heard that Witches "run around naked in the woods" or have "group sex."

We don't have group sex. Dammit.

On that wistful note I'm leaving it to you. There's a list of books you can read if you're interested in Wicca or in any other aspect of the religion, and some books on the Salem Witch trials.

Other than that, I'd like to leave you with a spell I first wrote in a magical book for kids and which I like to share with friends as we end our religious services:

> *May you live in happiness and harmony all your days,*
> *In peace with yourself and all people and creatures,*
> *In partnership with good spirits,*
> *In love with all good things of the earth, sea and sky.*
> *This spell is done with harm to none.*

Covens, Groups, and Witches:
Contributors to This Book

Incredible thanks to the following people and groups who contributed their favorite spells and rituals to keep love alive and kicking in an increasingly cynical world. HPs is the abbreviation for a High Priestess of a coven in the Wiccan religion, HP is the abbreviation for High Priest.

Web of Salem, a community-service group for Witches and Pagans

Clan of the Dragon, Kerowyn Silverdrake, HPs, Salem

Jane Raeburn, HPs, and Maine Pagan Resources. Jane is the author of "Jane's Tidings," a popular news column for Witches and Pagans that appears in many Pagan publications and websites. Jane keeps us up on the latest developments, whether they're serious or downright strange.

Maine Pagan Resources is a networking group. They publish a newsletter, the *Earth Tides Pagan Network News,* for eleven dollars a year. EPN, PO Box 161, East Winthrop, ME 04343. They also have a Maine Pagan Mailing List for e-mail. To subscribe, send a message to listmom@maine.rr.com with SUBSCRIBE MEP in the body of the message. See their web page at http://home.maine.rr.com/mepagan/

Cassius Julianus, HP, and the Julian Society, PO Box 622, Nashua, NH 03063

The Julian Society works toward the restoration of Pagan religious rites and making Paganism more respected, effective, and influential in the modern world. The Society is a working fraternal order, with its teaching inspired by Julian, the last Pagan emperor of Rome. The Society maintains a website at www.geocities.com/Athens/Acropolis/1568/index.html

Nova Roma is an organization dedicated to the study and restoration of ancient Roman culture. They are a historical re-creation society, a pagan religious organization, a classical studies group, and a sovereign "micronation" dedicated to re-creating the best of classical Pagan Rome through the practice of the Roman Virtues and the *Religio Romana*. This very interesting group maintains a website at http://www.novaroma.org, and publishes a newsletter, the *Eagle*.

The Temple of Diana, Salem and Connecticut

The Sisterhood of Thalia, Salem, is a group that honors Thalia, the muse of comedy. Lady Moira Keltic Thanyou, HPs and General Jokester. The group can be reached through having an out-of-body-experience while listening to Weird Al Yankovic records.

Artemisia Botanicals, Teri Kalgren, owner, 102 Wharf Street, Salem, MA 01970

Lilith McLelland, HPs, can be reached through writing Carol Publishing, or at missmoon@ix.netcom.com. No unsolicited Jehovah's Witnesses, please. All offers of cybersex cheerfully rejected.

Reading List

For More Information on Witchcraft, Wicca, and Paganism

Wicca for the Solitary Practitioner, Scott Cunningham, Llewellyn, 1989
The Rebirth of Witchcraft, Doreen Valiente, Robert Hale Ltd., 1989
Witchcraft Today, Gerald Gardner, Magickal Childe, 1989
The Golden Bough, Sir James George Frazer, Macmillan, 1922
Positive Magic, Marion Weinstien, Phoenix Publishing, 1978
The Power of the Witch, Laurie Cabot, Delacorte, 1989
Two Orations of the Emperor Julian, Thomas Taylor, Kessinger Pub., 1991
Julian, Gore Vidal, Ballantine, 1986

For Pagan Kids, Ages 10–16

Spellcraft, A Primer for the Young Magician, Lilith McLelland, Eschaton, 1997

On the Salem Witch Trials

A Delusion of Satan, Frances Hill, Doubleday, 1995
Salem Possessed, Paul Boyer and Stephen Nissenbaum, Harvard University Press, 1979
The Devil in Massachusetts, Marion Starkey, Doubleday, 1949